PROSPERITY THINKING

DEVELOPING THE MINDSET
FOR ATTRACTING
INFINITE RICHES

RYUHO OKAWA
FOUNDER OF HAPPY SCIENCE

Contents

CHAPTER TWO
How to Keep Away Spirits of Poverty

CHAPTER THREE

Prosperity Thinking

CHAPTER FOUR
Become Closer toward the God of Prosperity

Preface

There is a widespread tendency in this world to see those who succeed and accumulate wealth in a negative light. This is represented by the analogy of crabs in the lower part of a bucket using their pincers to pull down the one that tries to escape. What would happen if we develop a culture where the crab that succeeds in escaping teaches the other crabs how to do the same, thus helping them escape, one after another? There would be a procession of successful individuals emerging one after another.

I believe in equal opportunities because it leads to prosperity that comes from freedom. However, I do not necessarily approve of equal results, which is the rationalization of jealousy. If a world is created where people who succeed by putting effort and getting wisdom get condemned and where lazy people get benefits, it will certainly bring down the moral of society.

Do not use the words, "reducing inequalities" as an excuse to revive the ghost of Marx. A healthy inequality encourages others, providing society with motivation and energy. The starting point of prosperity lies in having a positive attitude toward prosperity.

Ryuho Okawa
National Teacher
January 17, 2012

Chapter One

Let's Achieve Success

1

It is Good to Become Rich

Do you have a sense of guilt toward wealth?

The theme of this chapter is, "Let's Achieve Success." There are many types of people among the readers and the subject of success is extremely broad, so I could go on forever if I were to talk about it in the general sense.

Therefore, this may sound somewhat unusual, but I would like to talk about how to make money and how to get rich.

There will, of course, be some who won't get rich despite reading this chapter. But there will be about the same percentage of people who will get wealthy as the people who recover from illness by listening to my lectures.

If we narrow our definition of the word *success* as "getting rich," then the most important mindset is, "don't reject wealth."

There are quite a number of religious people who have a sense of guilt toward wealth. In religions that existed 2,000 years ago or earlier, including Christianity, Buddhism and other religions, wealth was often taught as such and ultimately became synonymous with the devil.

It's definitely true that wealth has this aspect. There are many cases in which wealth or money can delude you. So, wealth could be a path to your downfall.

However, another path, the path to progress and prosperity, is also open to us. A person who finds success through wealth chooses this path; whether or not a person chooses this path depends on his lifestyle and aspirations.

Therefore, if I were straightforwardly asked whether the thought of disapproving wealth, as in the teachings of early Buddhism and Christianity, is correct in the modern age, I would have to say, "No."

Today, there are many companies starting up, with a steady stream of them becoming big businesses and employing tens or hundreds of thousands of people. With the emergence of these huge businesses, new jobs are being created and the employees are able to provide for their families by working there. Many people have been able to create large businesses within their own lifetimes.

For example, there is the Microsoft billionaire, Bill Gates, as well as many people who have created major businesses in Japan. If we rejected all these businesses and thought of all the heads of major businesses as Satans from Hell, then the people living off their salaries earned by working there would be minions of those Satans.

However, that's not the case. If you want to make the world affluent, make people happy and get wealthy from work that actually accomplishes these goals without harming the world, then that's not a bad thing.

Treating successful people as evil is A mistaken concept of left-wing ideology

As I have mentioned, one may call wealth evil, disapproving of it due to the religious sense of guilt. Or, he may think from a Marxist left-wing ideology that all people who make money are evil and that there are many who are poor and unhappy because such people exist.

Recently, such thinking has come up again with the phrase, "unequal society" being used to denigrate economic inequality.

Even on television, there are many programs closely covering and reporting on the homeless. But there have always been homeless people.

Nowadays, the idea that the rich are evil and the poor are righteous does not pass. Wisdom and effort are necessary for attaining success. If we deny such wisdom and effort, the world will become full of lazy people.

There is something wrong in a society where one cannot succeed despite giving his best efforts. Such society is one with no opportunities and one in which opportunities are not given equally.

That's why I am advocating the need for equal opportunities. A society is indeed harsh if there is no opportunity given to start businesses in the first place or if there is no prospect of success in life unless one is born into the aristocracy or, as in the old days, the family of a feudal lord.

Meanwhile, I believe that a good society is one in which opportunities are given equally and paths open before us through individual effort, diligence and resourcefulness.

Thus, disparity is inevitable. However, a world where people are envious of those who have found success or treat them as evil just because this disparity exists is not good. We should embrace such people and acknowledge their excellence.

There will always be people who fail no matter what, so I think certain safety nets or relief measures are necessary to guarantee a minimum standard of living at the national and community levels.

At the same time, it is important that those who succeed demonstrate chivalry by giving back to society and that successful companies increase their number of employees.

Measures for dealing with unemployment are not

only for the government to implement. Companies, too, should make an effort to give back to society. For example, by establishing new factories in regions where there are no employment opportunities.

The idea, "money is time" changed my life

I, myself, had an experience that changed my way of thinking when I was young.

When I was a teenager, I harbored the same belief I mentioned earlier of fundamental religions, the idea of fundamental Buddhism and Christianity that one cannot serve both wealth and God. This idea was that of honesty and poverty; I thought that a poor and pure life was the right way to live.

That mindset changed when I learnt of the expression "money is time," the reverse of the saying, "time is money." I learnt of this way of thinking when I was about 20 and was struck by the truth to it.

"Money is time" [time can be bought with money] means that by having money you can make progress with your work and that expanding your business becomes easier.

Even with my work, there is a limit to what I can do alone, but if there are others to help, the scope of my work can be broadened.

If we take reading books as an example, going to a big bookstore to buy books may be fun, but it's basically half a day's work. However, if I have the money to employ a secretary, I can have him go buy books from the bookstore for me. That will save me half a day. I can then use that time to read even more books.

This holds true for work as well. If you have a lot of capital, you can get through your work quickly.

This is also true for Happy Science. If we have an accumulation of funds, we can build many branches or build temples to hold seminars in, all over Japan. We can also do overseas missionary work. This way we can essentially shorten the time we take to do things. So, it is true, in a sense, that one can buy time with money.

Therefore, if you have worthy goals and motives in the work you are trying to do and you work hard for the benefit of society, then you may find that both "time is money" and "money is time" are true for you.

In this way, my life actually changed considerably by changing my way of thinking when I was young.

Happy Science accepts wealth achieved Through right work

If you have, from the start, an internal sense of guilt toward wealth, you will not become rich. This is because you, yourself, believe that becoming wealthy is akin to going to Hell and becoming a friend of devils. In such situation, you will fail, for some reason, no matter how hard you try.

For example, if you manage a company, it will go bankrupt. This is because you feel that you will not be able to go to Heaven if you don't fail. Since you feel that you can go to Heaven if you go bankrupt and become penniless, but that you will go to Hell if you make money, you will let yourself make bad moves and run the company into the ground.

Even though it can't be helped for the company president to become penniless as a result of going out of business, there are usually employees at a company. Whether there be 10, 30 or 100 employees, the head is responsible for looking after the livelihoods of those employees and their families.

What happens to the company president himself is of less concern; the bankruptcy of the company is a grave matter for the people working there. Therefore, bankruptcy is a bad thing.

Right work consists of selling the company's goods and products to make a profit, keeping the company in the black and being able to regularly pay the employees' salaries. Right work should also involve giving the employees hope and having them embrace this vision of the future. This is the right management policy. This is how it must be.

Of course, you hear many nasty stories about making money and it seems that people blinded by money turn to crime and make headlines in the newspaper daily. Because there is the danger of turning to crime if one thinks only of gaining money quickly and easily, we should probably consider the aforementioned words of the ancient religions to be warnings against such actions.

Meanwhile at Happy Science, we put forth the idea, "Wealth which is properly gained through hard work, use of wisdom and through effort and diligence, is not to be denied." This seems to be a new concept, even for people overseas.

The people of Asian and African nations, in particular, read my books translated into English and their national languages. They apparently are thinking whether they could engage in building their country based on these teachings, whether they could use the teachings to lead their country and introduce Japan's secret of success.

Money for making people happy is good

I'll say it again: you will not become rich if you deny wealth, so you should correct this tendency in your thinking.

You should think that wealth used for good things is good wealth and that value created through right effort and diligence, use of wisdom and doing right work is correct.

You should not think that making money is the equivalent of doing something bad.

For example, it's no good to think while making things at your factory, "The people who buy our products will become unhappy. Yet, I want to make money." Instead, you should pray in your mind as you work and believe that they will gain happiness by using your products.

It's important for you to want to make your products better than those of other companies and to want those who use them to be happy.

Several years ago, there was an incident where a company dishonestly resold "tainted rice"—rice imported for non-food products which was partly moldy—under the pretext of food. If you do something like this just to make money, you will immediately lose trust.

The company in question may have felt that it was a bit of a waste and perhaps thought it would be OK if the moldy parts were removed.

However, the motives are not pure of someone who would purposely resell such rice just because there is an opportunity to make money. Because food products have a direct bearing on people's health, the thought of wanting to profit by selling something that will harm people's health is a problem, indeed. You must restrain yourself from doing such things.

This lust for money will lead you to corruption. And it is clearly evil to knowingly engage in such actions.

On the other hand, there are people in the world who strive for health-conscious reasons to offer a product that will improve the health of those who eat it. However, once something like the tainted rice incident becomes widely known, rice itself will not be consumed as often and all rice farmers will be adversely affected. Such misconduct is unforgivable because honest, hard-working people are greatly affected by this.

In that sense, it is OK to think that making money is good if you are always aiming to benefit society in motive or result. Ensuring that you have a right motive is particularly important.

Thus, you should consider money that creates time to be good as is money for making people happy. This is the first point I would like to make.

2

The Maximum Self-realization

Money, social standing and reputation are not Things you can get by wanting

Since there are so many different jobs in the world, it's difficult to speak in general, but the things that everyone in the world desires such as money, social standing and reputation aren't things you can get by just wanting. If you have a job that is suitable to attaining these things, then those around you will help you to do so in good order.

For example, even if you don't think about getting a promotion, if you do your work properly, those around you will appreciate it and your social standing will naturally improve. Furthermore, even if you don't think about gaining money, if you are doing good work to create high added value, then your company's revenue will increase and your salary will also naturally go up. In this way, the environment around you will change.

It may sound strange, but that's how it really goes. There's no need for you to seek these things; you will be given these things as a result.

In any case, what is fitting for a person will gravitate toward him. The person in question does not know what is fitting for him, but the people around him and in the world do.

In terms of a company, for example, the size the company will attain is determined by the standing of that company in the eyes of the world. The world comprehensively appraises that company's work and naturally determines the extent to which that company will expand. A company that the world wants to expand more will gain more customers and further increase in size. That's the way it is.

Therefore, even if you don't pursue it, you will be given the standing to which you are suited.

If your salary is inappropriately large, your social standing too high or your reputation too great, the "principle of adjustment" will come into play. And as a result, you will need to reflect on yourself.

For example, even if you become rich for the time being, you may find yourself using up that money in some way. You may lose money on investment or what has been profitable until that point may no longer be by some sort of environmental change and, as a result, be eliminated.

Even if all of your efforts seemed to have been going well by a favorable wind, things may go badly when this tailwind stops blowing.

However, if your work really is something that society

appreciates and needs, you can overcome economic fluctuations and survive. Businesses that are always thinking about what the world needs and caring about their customers will continue to grow regardless of the surroundings.

This is also the case in terms of getting promoted within a company, so there is no need to think about your own advancement. If you are constantly working while bearing in mind the company's development and the happiness you can bring to your customers and the people who interact with the company through your work, then your social standing and income will naturally improve.

Humans have a tendency to become self-centered, so you have to be careful. If you become self-centered, you will become blind and lose your understanding of the matters around you.

You should know that the world will evaluate you correctly and go about your daily work with diligence.

Happy people don't have much time
To think about themselves

Let's move away from the topic of success and turn to the topic of happiness in general.

When you look back on the events of a day, people who spend a lot of the day thinking only about themselves are not very happy. People who only think about themselves are, more or less, unhappy.

Conversely, happy people don't really think about themselves. They don't have much time to think about themselves because they are always thinking about what they can do for others.

Of course, even those people will think about themselves a little when they take time for self-reflection, but unhappy people think about themselves from morning to night. They think the world revolves around them, coming up with reasons and excuses for their unhappiness and badmouthing people who they feel are responsible for making them unhappy. This is the characteristic of unhappy people.

If you add up the amount of time in a day you spend thinking about yourself, you will know roughly whether you are unhappy or not. People who always think about themselves are, sorry to say, unhappy.

Take a housewife for example. She may suddenly realize that she has spent a long time thinking not about herself, but about her husband and children, or her neighbors and acquaintances. If so, she is a happy person. But if she thinks mainly about herself, she is more likely to be unhappy.

People who are truly happy or who have successfully achieved self-realization seldom think about their own issues.

You cannot achieve the maximum self-realization if you are concerned only about yourself.

Ultimately, the maximum self-realization refers to how much you can contribute to society. Thus, the mind of people who have achieved self-realization is often filled with thoughts about the world and society.

Actually, people can say they are on the path to maximum self-realization when they are able to do so. That's what I would like to say.

Whether we're on the topic of happiness or success, people who have egocentric thoughts cannot be called happy or successful people. People who don't spend much time thinking about themselves are, in fact, often happy and successful.

I would especially like the women, in particular, to think carefully about this. Do you have a miserable self-image when you are at home? Or are you overwhelmed by fear? Is your mind full of dark thoughts such as fear of the future, fear of being rejected or not being accepted by others, or fear of being humiliated? Think about this carefully.

The courage to fight the fear of the unknown is A talent of business managers

There is also something I'd like to say about business managers.

Humans are creatures that are easily scared, but you need the courage to fight the fear of the future and fear of the unknown in order to succeed as business managers.

Everyone is scared of the unknown or unfamiliar. However, people who have the courage to fight and overcome this fear of the unknown have the talent to be business managers.

You can't see what's ahead, so you may waver in deciding the direction in which you should proceed. There are many factors involved in making such decisions, including your advancement, your salary or the fate of the company. It is extremely important, however, to win the battle against that fear of the unknown.

You need wisdom and courage to overcome this fear. You also need to be diligent on a daily basis. Wisdom, courage and an attitude of constant diligence are important.

We are faced with pitfalls everywhere in life. We face many potential sources of failure in life.

But from a wider perspective, there is something you can trust in: help will always come to those who are honest and diligent, whether they are in a crisis, are caught in a trap or are going through hardships.

There will always be a helping hand for those who are not two-faced but are honest and diligent, for those who put forth their best effort whether others are watching or not. They will always receive a helping hand, should they fall into a pitfall, be caught in a trap or on the verge of failure.

Believe me, the world is not blind. Those around you are watching carefully. There is no doubt that they are watching, with eyes as accurate as God's, whether a person is egotistical and only living for himself or whether the person has high goals and is always working hard and being diligent.

There is a clear difference between an effort to make yourself look as if you are working hard and an effort that comes from your heart.

In that sense, seen from a wider perspective, although the world may be mistaken in the short-term, it will virtually never be mistaken in the long-term. Therefore, if you or your company has wisdom, has courage, works hard and is diligent, all for the right vision, you will be evaluated accordingly.

However, there will, of course, be times when the company's business won't go well despite your best efforts due to various influences, such as the political climate and foreign relations. Also, depending on the period, you may encounter a time when the industries in vogue change and your business won't do well. In such times, though, it is important to believe, "When one door closes, another will certainly open."

Generally speaking, you should know that a path will always open to those who work hard, believing in a bright future.

Wish for great success, don't set your own limits

It is extremely important not to think on a small scale. If your intentions are good and will make the people of the world happy, please think on a large scale, whether it be company work or individual work. Think about great success.

For example, a person wants to become a writer and write novels. In that case, he should not be self-limiting by thinking, "I would be happy if I sold a few thousand copies, since good books generally don't sell too well." If it really is a good piece of work, then he should hope that hundreds of thousands or millions of people read it.

I, myself, have always thought in this manner, so that's the way things are for me now. What's more, not millions but hundreds of millions of people read my books.

Furthermore, the number of books I have put out has topped 800 [as of the end of 2011]*. It happened before I knew it. I don't mean to talk big, but when I consider this volume of work that I have produced, I've really worked hard these twenty-something years.

Even though things have changed over these twenty-something years, I always did my utmost and never slacked off. That's how I managed to write so many books.

Moreover, only about 10 percent of what I've studied are written in the books. There is about 90 percent of what I've accumulated that has not been written in the books yet.

In that sense, I have always had the approach that I will never write the same thing over, leading to a book that is reduced in quality and then have readers say the book was a waste of time and money.

The people in the world tend to look down on new religions, but I cannot bear the idea that the amount of study I've done could be less than that of other authors and critics. I have always worked hard and diligently for over 30 years, since I was around 20. That's how much knowledge I have accumulated.

It's thanks to this that I have delivered over 1,600 lectures in twenty-something years [as of the end of 2011]†. I have never given the same lecture twice. This is not an easy achievement. Even influential critics may constantly reiterate the same point during the course of a year. Politicians who appear to be good public speakers may reuse the same speech in front of different train stations.

Saying something different every time and continually putting out different books each year are not actually things you can do unless you put in considerable effort behind the scenes.

At the basis of that is a strong passion to share the Truth with billions of people. I don't know the form in which the Truth will reach each person. Thus, I continue to strive to create every possible entrance to the Truth, so that it will always reach someone out there.

As a result, my books sell like those of best-selling authors, but I believe people who read them don't ever feel that they have wasted their money.

Please note that I don't receive royalties from my books distributed within the Happy Science group. I donate the full amount to the group. I used to receive royalties as other writers in the world do for the books sold in bookstores, but now I don't. The royalties are all poured back into the group.

---

* As of June 2015, the author has published over 1,900 books.

† The author has given more than 2,300 lectures since establishing Happy Science in 1986.

Furthermore, I also function as a *daikokuten* or Angel of Wealth [a person who financially supports a religious order], financially supporting the group by donating part of my income to scholarships and the construction of the Ryuho Okawa Memorial Hall at the Happy Science Academy.

Having money is a great thing in the sense that you can use it freely for good purposes. I think it is good for you, whether it be as an individual or a company, to grow your business with the idea of wanting to do an honest job, wanting to increase your income, wanting to use that money for the right causes and wanting to produce extra funds for that purpose.

3

Winning an All-out Battle of Human vs. Human

People with power of persuasion will Succeed in any job

Lastly, I'd like to add just one more point.

Persuading another person is an all-out battle of human vs. human. A person's capacity can be measured when he persuades another person.

You cannot be bad at making money if you have power of persuasion. It is generally said that in a company, there is about a hundred-fold difference between the business capability of a sales staff and that of the company president. That shows in the differences between their salaries and their social standings, but ultimately, the difference is one between their capabilities as human beings.

Thus, it is generally said that there is about a hundred-fold difference between the company president negotiating by giving a sales pitch himself and a salesperson giving a sales pitch. A person with power of persuasion has comprehensive capabilities as a human being.

Persuading others is an all-out battle. It's an all-out battle incorporating elements such as past experience, stores of knowledge, ability to judge character, intuition, inspiration, the power of guardian and guiding spirits and the power of colleagues. The actual results reflect all of these intangible factors which are at work.

This is why I have no doubt that people with power of persuasion will succeed in any job. They will certainly succeed, even if they were to switch careers or start a business.

Those with power of persuasion will succeed in whatever they do. Such powers reflect those people's ability to do work. Meanwhile, people with no power of persuasion will struggle, no matter what they do. Such ability applies to everything.

Make efforts with sincerity as your motto

People who do their job well get their work done very quickly. They finish their work in a flash, so they can help others or take on a new challenge by using their free time.

A person's ability to do work manifests in the same way, no matter what he does. If a person believes that he has 100 times the power of persuasion of others and if this is in fact true, then that person can become a company president. There's no doubt about it. If such person's power of persuasion is 100 times that of the average person, then the capable person, whether a man or a woman, has what it takes to become a company president.

You should feel that persuading someone is an opportunity to test yourself and give it your best.

When you do so, it's particularly important to be sincere. Do not wish to succeed by fooling or deceiving someone. At work, for example, you must not fool or deceive a customer into buying a bad product. You won't be able to keep up that sort of action for long. Also, if your superior finds out that you are doing something like that, you will be fired.

Therefore, make efforts with sincerity as your motto. If you can do so, you can apply it to all aspects of life.

I'd like you to bear this in mind.

Don't set limits to your great aspirations

Don't set limits to your great aspirations. There are many people who can't help but think small.

There was a book, which I read some time ago, that told the following humorous anecdote.

Once upon a time, there was a person fishing for trout in a river. When he caught a small trout, he put it in his fish basket, but when he caught a big one, he threw it back in the water.

Someone who saw this thought it was strange and wondered why he would do such a thing. When he asked, the fisherman replied, "Our frying pan is only 25 centimeters [about 10 inches] in diameter, so we can't cook trout bigger than that. That's why I release the big trout when I catch them and only take the little ones home."

The book had such humorous anecdote. In fact, many of you often do the same thing. There are many who only take home the "small fish" and throw away the "big fish," believing you can't cook them in your frying pans.

If that's the case, you should get a bigger frying pan. Please buy "a big frying pan."

You may be placing limits on yourself in terms of your capabilities or the type of work which you are capable of handling, but this makes you just like the person I mentioned—a person who releases the big fish and keeps the little ones to suit his frying pan.

There are many people in the world who do this. The important thing is to have a big frying pan ready. I would like you to cook a big fish in a big frying pan. Please don't think about things only to suit the size of your frying pan.

Don't put limits on yourself by saying, "I don't need fish that are bigger than 25 cm." Think about getting a bigger frying pan.

That is what I ask of you.

Chapter Two

How to Keep Away
Spirits of Poverty

1

Miracles of Attracting Wealth

Happy Science is a group that can perform Many and all sorts of miracles

There are all kinds of miracles occurring at Happy Science. Now, as one kind of category for miracles, I'd like to perform miracles related to wealth.

There are miracles in which illness is healed and miracles in which someone suddenly does well in his studies. And there's the miracle of improving interpersonal relationships. In fact, this world is filled with all kinds of miracles and our group has also seen many miracles. But one more category of miracle that must not be forgotten is the miracle of attracting wealth. Happy Science is a group that can perform miracles of attracting wealth.

This is a topic that I touch upon occasionally, but I feel that so far most of you who have been listening have yet to fully attain enlightenment regarding this. I feel like only a few of you really understands. There seems to be many people who, even when they listen to my lectures, just let the words pass right over their heads. Or, even when reading my books, they just sort of skim through, thinking, "I guess these kinds of miracles really do happen out there in the world," all the while never realizing that I'm talking about them, too.

I'm sorry to say that the learning ability of Happy Science followers in the arena of enlightenment regarding wealth is still actually one-hundredth of what it should be.

There are a lot of people who still think miracles related to wealth are for other people and say, "Maybe there are people in the world who are chosen by God or Buddha to become rich. I guess there are sometimes people who are born as *daikokuten* or Angels of Wealth and are blessed with that kind of mission. But this has nothing to do with me."

However, this line of thought is wrong. Just as you can receive the miracle of healing by learning the laws of the mind through Happy Science and living a way of life that doesn't attract malicious spirits, miracles related to wealth are also ruled by certain laws.

Mastering "the laws to attract wealth" is One form of attaining enlightenment

Reports of miracles on healing appear in things like Happy Science monthlies* from time to time. But the cases

---

* See the *About Happy Science* section near the end of this book.

reported are only a small amount, the tip of an iceberg. The truth is, the more impossible a miracle may seem or the more likely people would say, "No way, that could never happen," the more likely it is for such a miracle to go unwritten. The cases that we actually should write up are the ones that don't get written, but cases where a person could've easily gotten better without a miracle are the ones that generally get written up.

For example, one story of an amazing miracle is as follows. A person suffered a cerebral contusion in an accident. His skull was fractured, the frontal lobe of the brain was damaged beyond recognition and the brain wouldn't stop hemorrhaging. Doctors said, "We don't know if this person's life can be saved or not. We need to perform a craniotomy right away."

That night, a lecturer at one of the Happy Science temples conducted a ritual prayer wishing for this person's recovery. When the doctors took more X-ray photographs in preparation for the surgery the next morning, the brain hemorrhage had stopped. They decided not to perform the surgery and instead decided to wait and see how things went. The victim recovered at an amazing speed. His skull restored its original shape in a short amount of time. There were absolutely no aftereffects. This kind of thing actually happens.

However, this story didn't appear in any of the monthlies for several years. It wasn't announced in any way. Happy Science is the kind of group that doesn't mind letting such a great miracle go unnoticed. In fact, even I, master of Happy Science, didn't hear about it until several years after the event.

Any other religion would definitely and immediately use this kind of story in advertisements and promotions for their religious order. This is the usual case, but in our case, everyone kept quiet about it and hid it for several years, until one day the master happened to hear about it by some coincidence.

Normally, this kind of recovery can't happen. The victim suffered a fractured skull and cerebral contusions at a dangerous level, but he recovered without surgery and had no aftereffects whatsoever.

There were some cases where a cancer was cured in a single evening through the ritual prayers of Happy Science. This is amazing, too, but there might be people who think, "Maybe the cancer diagnosis was actually just an error in the X-ray analysis."

However, there's absolutely no way you could say that "recovering from a skull fracture and cerebral contusions" was an error in the X-ray analysis. The ritual prayers at Happy Science have the power to "move continents."

Nevertheless, I must say that in the past, Happy Science used to be a group that wasn't good at putting these kinds of amazing miracles done by prayer, which actually occurred, to use in a skillful way. Apparently, Happy Science staff members used to have a level of information awareness that was so low, they couldn't imagine what would happen if they told people about these miracles. They used to work only on the level of the average office worker or civil servant, having the attitude of working very hard, but only on jobs assigned to them.

This is proof that, in truth, they hadn't yet fully mastered the laws to attract wealth which I will talk about later. There are many different kinds of enlightenment; mastering the laws to attract wealth is one form of attaining enlightenment. People who haven't mastered these laws won't recognize or realize that there's an innate potential for them to be able to increase supporters and income. This is the reality.

2

How to Avoid Being Possessed by Spirits of Poverty

Are you possessed by a spirit of poverty?

In this world, there are people who, although being honest, upright and very good people, think they're doing good work but are actually totally off the mark. Such people, whether they work at a company or try to sell things on their own, are just scooping water in their sieves or trying to get water using a bucket that has a hole in it. They let opportunities slip away, even if they were to come face to face with important customers and customers who are actually ready to order merchandise.

For example, there are people who will miss a rare chance to meet with the key person in the company they're having negotiations with. Instead, they work themselves to the bone negotiating with someone who isn't the key person, by which I mean someone who doesn't hold the key to making important decisions. This kind of person contacts people who can't really make any decisions even if they listen to what you have to say, asking them for important things many, many times.

There are people who work hard in meeting, time after time, with people who not only don't possess the authority to make decisions, but who have absolutely no motivation to communicate the discussion to his superiors. On the contrary, they never go to anyone with any real authority or anyone who can understand the topic at hand. Such are the kind of people who miss opportunities to rise in status or increase their incomes.

There are different ways to describe these people, all according to their own individual traits, but overall you could say that they haven't yet mastered the laws to attract wealth. Put differently, you could also say, "Maybe you're possessed by a spirit of poverty*. You should check carefully to see if a spirit of poverty is possessing you personally or your company as a whole." This is what I want to say.

Spirits of poverty not only possesses individuals, But also companies and nations

If someone says, "The more I work, the less I seem to succeed financially and the heavier my loans get" then there's an extremely high chance that the person, or that person's company, is possessed by a spirit of poverty.

---

* A spirit that brings poverty, illness or accidents to people.

Also, there are cases when an entire nation is possessed by a spirit of poverty. This is true of Japan now [at the time of the lecture]. The nation of Japan is possessed by a spirit of poverty.

So, the question is, "How do you save the nation when its top leader is possessed by a spirit of poverty?" This is the very question that I'm tackling right now. If you get rid of the leader targeted by that spirit of poverty, I'm sure the problem would resolve itself somehow. But the leader isn't going anywhere anytime soon.

Right now, the leader of this nation is dragging its people down. Happy Science is shining light on the nation from below, but shining from below is a tough job. When shining light from below, it takes a bit of time to make the spirit of poverty realize that it's hot in order to drive it out. There isn't much we can do, since there are so many people who are supporting that spirit of poverty [the leader of the nation].

Getting rid of him would be simple if only the majority of the people weren't supporting him. But the thing is, there are so many people supporting this spirit of poverty. The reason is because their mind is in tune with that of the spirit. People share the same state of mind and view themselves as being of the same kind. That's why they support him. Thus, these people will become poor, too.

Why do nations fall into financial deficit and become poor? This is because the work that the government does isn't making the people wealthier. It's because the government isn't doing things to let its people gain wealth. It's because the work that the government is doing is making its people poor. This is obvious.

There are people who, when faced with the decision to choose one of two options, have the tendency to make the wrong choice or to decide on the route that leads to loss. There are actually a lot of people in the world who repeatedly lose these fifty-fifty bets. In most cases, choices come down to things like "right or left" or "yes or no"; basically, it's one or the other. Despite so, there are a certain share of people who have the tendency to choose the option opposite from the correct one, who always chooses the wrong option. The sad thing is that the people who support spirits of poverty will share the same fate.

The same thing is true of companies. If a company president is possessed by a spirit of poverty or if a company president is someone who could be called an embodiment of a spirit of poverty, then saving that company won't be an easy task. Even if one of his subordinates is an embodiment of a god of luck, getting rid of the negativity that the spirit of poverty generates won't be easy unless the subordinate works extremely hard.

Spirits of poverty are, in truth, the spirits of people Like business owners who committed suicide

Spirits of poverty actually exist in this world. I generally teach, "Devils and evil spirits exist in the world." In the other world, there really are spirits who make it their "job" to make other people ill, cause accidents on them and make them suffer.

These spirits used to be unhappy people when they were alive in this world. When such people die and become spiritual beings in the other world, though happiness is out of their reach, they at least feel something similar to contentment if they can make other people feel unhappy. They feel, "Ah, now you're unhappy, too!"

They don't wish for their own happiness, but they believe their unhappiness fades when they mass-produce unhappiness for other people. Seeing a lot of people become unhappy makes them feel as if they are happy after all. There really are spirits like this who live in that kind of illusion; they actually are working behind the scenes. One type of such spirits is the so-called "spirits of poverty" which bring unhappiness in the economic sense.

As for where these spirits of poverty come from, most of them used to be people who, while they were living in this world, ran some kind of business on their own only to have their company go bankrupt. They met a tragic end, such as suicide by hanging or having their families split up and their lives turned upside down. Such people turn into what we call spirits of poverty.

If one of these gods possesses a company, that company will go under. If a spirit of poverty possesses people he knew while he was alive, the victims' companies would also go under just as his company did.

This kind of thing happens often. Just as there are cases when spirits of poverty go after the people he knew in life, there are also cases in which the spirits remain attached to a certain location. In such cases, people who try to run a business there or rent a house and try to sell things there will always fail.

There are places where businesses fail, one after another. If a factory pops up, it goes bust. If a store pops up, it goes bankrupt. This might sound like I'm talking about *feng shui* or something, but you have to be careful because there really are places where spirits of poverty have become earth-bound spirits.

People become similar to the people they respect

Then, what kind of countermeasures should you take against spirits of poverty? Basically speaking, possession by spirits of poverty is based on the laws of the mind that I've been teaching. Spirits in the other world and people living in this world who are similar are bound together by the Law of Same Wavelengths' Attraction. Entities of the same kind always connect, so if a person living in this world has the state of mind with a wavelength that attracts a spirit of poverty, then the spirit will respond to that wavelength.

This is completely different from the case wherein someone who actually has money loves spirits of poverty and invokes them coercively. If you pray daily, "Spirits of poverty, come to me. Spirits of poverty, come to me," then spirits of poverty will most likely come to you. There's nothing you can do about people who knowingly call spirits of poverty. But setting aside such kind of curious people, the truth is that most people are in tune with the gods of poverty without even knowing it.

Why are people in tune without even knowing it? One of the causes you will find is the family environment such people had up until they reached adulthood. There are a lot of people who had parents who struggled financially during their childhood. In postwar Japan, I imagine that there were many parents who had severe financial difficulties, since there were a lot of cases of bankruptcy and unemployment. However, when the parents tell their children about this, in many cases, the story of their financial troubles transforms into a kind of "heroic legend."

Some children are made to believe, "My parents failed in their businesses, again and again, so I guess people can't live their lives without suffering," by the age of 20. The more they respect their parents, the stronger their tendency to follow their parents' footsteps.

Children unconsciously follow the examples of their parents. Yes, the experience of poverty is a very valuable thing, but if you idolize it and imprint it into your children as if it were some sort of amazing legend, they'll end up making similar mistakes. You have to be careful of things like this. This is an example of unconsciously invoking the spirits of poverty.

Of course, your attitude and mindset after you grow up and become an adult are factors, too. In the political sphere, I'm against left-wing ideology. Previously, I recorded a spiritual message from Marx [see Chapter 1 from *Marx, Mao Zedong no Spiritual Message* (Spiritual Messages from Marx and Mao Zedong) (Tokyo: IRH Press, 2010)]. In this message, we revealed that Marx, the very founder of left-wing ideology, the very founder of communism, had been sleeping in the Unconscious Realm of Hell* for over 120 years. You'll only share

---

* A realm of Hell where people who preached wrong philosophy or religious teachings, and led a lot of people in the wrong direction fall after death.

a similar fate if you follow his ideology. So, you can see that who you respect or who you learn from is an extremely important issue.

In your childhood, you mainly watch your parents, so you get strongly influenced by them. But at some point, you have to shed this influence. If your parents are good parents, then it's fine to respect and imitate them. However, parents have aspects that should be respected and aspects that shouldn't be respected. When you become aware of an aspect of your parents that shouldn't be respected, you must not respect that aspect, but instead put someone who you should respect into that role and think to yourself, "I want to become just like that person."

There are many people who succeeded economically, who worked hard to better the world. If you select a person like that who is to your liking and continue to think, "I want to become like this person," your wavelength will gradually match that person's and will start to become like that person. People become similar to the people they respect. You'll gravitate toward the people you respect, so it's important to respect people who have achieved success.

The influence that parents have on you when you are a child is enormous. There's nothing anyone can do to change that. Even so, when you grow up and become an adult yourself, you must transcend the influence of your parents.

For example, you shouldn't try to justify making the same mistakes as your parents over and over again, saying, "Well, this is the way my parents did it" even after turning 30 or so. That's nothing more than trying to avoid taking responsibility. You're responsible for your own life after turning 30. It's no longer your parents' responsibility. When you hit 30, you must take responsibility for the view you have on finances, view on conducting business, view on working, view of society and opinion on politics.

Affirm the creation of wealth as something good And apply yourself diligently

Essentially, it's fine to be kind to weak people. The same can be said regarding the current Democratic Party of Japan administration [at the time of the lecture]. I think it's fine to be nice to weaker people. However, if you construct a society that enables anyone and everyone to become poor or weak, then the outcome would be an overall decline. If that happens, it'll actually become impossible to save weak people. Society will lose the very strength it needs to save weak people.

If you create a culture of hating and being jealous of people who work diligently, generate innovations and accumulate a large source of wealth or of people who succeed in managing companies, then people would start avoiding wealth and success since they don't want to be hated and envied by others. They would think, "As long as I'm just like everybody else, no one will think those things about me" and, therefore, lower their level of economic activity.

As a result, such a society will balance out at a low level. That low level will become the norm. If the top stops working hard and lowers their level, with the bottom remaining low, there would be no one to save the weaker people.

Financial deficit for the nation occurs due to reasons like this. Even though the government collects taxes, the country doesn't get wealthier since the government makes bad use of those taxes. It can't use tax money to make the country wealthy—thus, a financial deficit.

The same thing is true for companies. Deficits can be generated by the company president alone. So, in the end, if you don't affirm the creation of wealth as something good, you won't get wealthy. Please don't misunderstand this.

Old religions often refute wealth as being evil and Buddhism is no exception. There are many sayings regarding this in Buddhism and Christianity. But money-based economy had not developed all that much back when the founders of these religions were alive. Most of the early religious orders were poor. So, the teachings from those times aren't meant for the capitalist world that we live in today.

This is why there are many instances of people in older religions saying, "Wealth is evil" and other things as an excuse for their inability to adapt to the modern capitalist world. You must know this.

3

The Essence of Wealth

Are you benefiting and being appreciated By many people?

What is the essence of wealth? Simply put, it is to benefit a large number of people. This is an important point, so it bears repeating. The essence of wealth lies in whether or not something is benefiting a large number of people.

Looking at it from the opposite standpoint, benefiting a large number of people can be described as being appreciated by many people. A company would make a lot of money if it's appreciated for things, for instance, "Your company has helped us so much. Thanks to you, things have become incredibly convenient. Thank you very much."

For example, in Japan, we have the home delivery service. But in its initial development, it was forced to fight against the regulations set forth by governmental offices of that time, such as the Ministry of Posts and Telecommunications [currently the Ministry of Internal Affairs and Communications] and the Ministry of Transport [currently the Ministry of Land, Infrastructure, Transport and Tourism]. There were many trials regarding this service.

However, the appearance of the home delivery service meant that packages could generally reach their destinations anywhere in Japan within 24 hours, so delivering became extremely convenient. This is something for which a lot of people would definitely feel appreciative.

At that time, because the post office was not delivering packages on Saturdays and Sundays and there were basically over 100 "not-in-service days" in a year, it took forever for packages to arrive. Also, if you took a package to the post office for delivery, the workers there would often say, "This package is not within our specifications" and reject it. If that happened, you had no choice but to take it back home and repackage it. I've experienced this before and, let me say, it's not fun. It's irritating because you're getting refused even though *you* are the customer.

A postal worker at the post office will tell you, "The maximum measurements for length, width and height for packages are X, Y and Z," but no one would know until he actually goes to the post office. I simply had to say, "Oh, I see. This size is no good?" and take the package back home for repackaging. That was annoying, indeed.

Instead, if someone operating a home delivery service says, "Any size is fine. We'll pick it up at your house and deliver it for you. Your package will arrive on time within 24 hours," then that's surely something anyone would feel thankful for.

This is why it's only natural that a company that does this will make lots of money. It's a done deal. If a company that offers even better services pops up, then obviously the company with the better services would make even more money.

So, here's the bottom line: the essence of wealth is to benefit more and more people. Or, put in other words, the essence of wealth is to be respected or appreciated by more and more people. And if doing a job that's appreciated by more and more people is the essence of wealth, then it's odd to say, "Wealth is evil. The words 'be wealthy' are the whispering of the devil." There's absolutely nothing evil about doing a job that people appreciate.

The reason that older teachings rejected wealth is because times were different from ours. Today, if you do a job that makes the world a better place, you are appreciated and also make a lot of money. So, if people say, "We just aren't making any money," "Money isn't coming in" or "Our sales aren't going up," this means that they aren't doing the world much service. This means that people aren't all that appreciative of you, that you aren't really benefiting them.

Your revenue won't increase if you're working a job that doesn't benefit people. And if your business takes a turn for the worse, your company will be forced to make all sorts of reductions. Employees will become targets for layoffs and will end up losing their jobs.

An example of "customer discomfort"
Taken from a major airline

Next, I want to go into an incident that I've touched on before. A certain major airline in Japan did the following. I'm saying "a certain major airline" here, but since there are only two major airlines in Japan, I'm sure you can probably guess which one I'm talking about. It's the one that received financial support from the government several years ago.

I use this major airline frequently when I go on a missionary tour within Japan. This airline used to have the company rule, "Only four people per group can enter the special lounge." One time, our group had five people using that lounge. Happy Science got a call a few days later from the sales department of that airline and the message was, "The room is only available for up to four people, but your group had five people in the room. This is against the rules."

But if you think about it, there's something odd about that. Five customers should be better than four. Sales would be higher with five. So, in that sense, it should be fine if more people came into the room.

Traveling is not the same as a game of mahjong. If you're playing mahjong, then yes, only four people can play. Or, for example, a table at a Chinese restaurant may only be able to seat four people at a time. But an airline doesn't really have to think of things in units of four people like a mahjong game. Five people should be fine, too.

I spoke about this in one of my lectures. Sometime after that, a supplementary chair began to appear in the special lounge. The airline caught that information and changed its service immediately. I believe that's commendable. However, it's still true that, up until that time, the airline had laid down "a mahjong system" of four-people groups.

When you're traveling, there's no such thing as "always moving together in fours." Some groups will have more people and some will have less. It depends on how many people are traveling together with you. In our case, since we were told, "Having over four people is against the rules, so you have to have one person leave the room," we had one secretary who had to stand outside the lounge all alone until the airline started providing the supplementary chair. This secretary always had to stand outside the room. We couldn't regroup until the time of departure, when we boarded the plane.

If the lounge was full, I wouldn't have complaints. But the thing is, the room was usually almost empty. Even though the room had more than enough space overall, the rule of not accepting groups of over four people at a time continued unchallenged. What's more, this company ended up generating an enormous deficit. What I have to say about this is, I think it's wrong for this kind of company to receive a financial aid of around one trillion yen from the government.

It is the airline's way of thinking that is discomforting to the customer. "Objecting and complaining because too many customers came" is incredibly rude. It made me not want to ride on their planes again, but there aren't many options because there aren't many airlines. So, I only use the airline because I have to.

You can sit in the lounge with five people now, so I do commend the airline for catching the information in my lecture. Nevertheless, I must say that large companies do things like this with surprising frequency. But the private sector won't work if this sort of thing keeps occurring.

In addition, the following sort of thing kept occurring for a long time in the Japanese banking industry. Back when the Ministry of Finance was still known as the Ministry of the Treasury, it used to micromanage all sorts of decisions regarding the services banks provided. The ministry set forth all kinds of restrictions such as, "Matchboxes given out as free gifts can only be this specific size" and "Serving Japanese tea to customers is fine, but you can't serve coffee."

These kinds of things shouldn't be determined by government offices. The choice whether to serve coffee, black tea or Japanese tea should be something that the bank decides based on the transaction amount between the bank and the client. Banks should be allowed to provide top-class service to major clients and the appropriate level of service to smaller clients. In fact, just putting out a glass of water might be appropriate in some cases.

At that time, the government offices even decided whether banks could give away free tissue paper or not. But this isn't something that's decided by public officials. There are many examples where public officials did things like that and slowed down the growth of the economy. Ideas such as these that don't agree with the increase of wealth and ways of thinking that reject the increase of wealth find their way into your mind, so you have to be careful. You must have an affinity for wealth.

Do not deny wealth, And use the money collected for good things

Let me say this again: when you think about wealth, its starting point is to benefit more and more people. Or, put differently, being wealthy is to be appreciated by more and more people. This is the source of wealth.

From the standpoint of Buddha's Truth, this isn't wrong at all. If you benefit people and are appreciated by them, leading to an increase in revenue, then that's just perfect. What you should do then is to use the increased revenue for good things. "Buying a pile of machine guns and using them to support guerrilla fighters," "I can afford to buy a hundred machine guns with the money I've accumulated, so I'll pass these out to gang groups and initiate terrorist attacks" and similar thoughts are bad. But if you use accumulated money for good things instead of criminal acts, then that isn't a bad thing at all.

Several years ago, we said that we were going to build 200 local temples and we finished that project in the summer of 2010. In addition to that, we also have a couple dozen *shoshinkans* [main temples] and over 100 other facilities. It's wonderful to have things put out in physical form.

Happy Science local temples are lighthouses for their local regions. They are a shining light. They are lighthouses shining light around them. Constructing a local temple is a good way to use money. To have a local temple in an area means that, over the long term, our members in that area will spread the Truth to people there. The temple will be the power to bring those people together.

Thus, firmly increasing your revenue, or increasing profits in case of a company, and using that for good things is virtuous. Please don't deny wealth.

4

Bright, Active and Positive Way of Thinking

The spirit of Sontoku Ninomiya connects Studying and making money*

No matter what anyone says, if you think that a person is listening to the whispers of a spirit of poverty, then you must never take what that person is saying to heart, even if the person is the prime minister.

Right now, many people are being possessed by the spirits of poverty, especially those involved in education. This means that the people who are taught by them end up becoming poor. Those involved in education are devoting themselves wholeheartedly to that kind of misleading education.

It's extremely important to impart an entrepreneurial spirit to children. But if the teachers are infused with this spirit-of-poverty style of education, the people taught by

---

*Sontoku Ninomiya [1787-1856]: a Japanese agricultural leader and philosopher. Ninomiya was originally born into a family of peasants, but became famous after reconstructing the finances of a samurai family he served. He then went on to help restore more than 600 villages and feudal domains. Ninomiya is also known as the first person to practice capitalism in Japan.

those teachers are most likely to become poor. This isn't good at all.

Right now, the Happiness Realization Party* has a small statue of Sontoku Ninomiya reading my book, *The Manifesto of the Happiness Realization Party* [Tokyo: Happy Science, 2014]. There used to be a small statue of Sontoku Ninomiya in almost every elementary school in Japan. The school I went to had one, too.

Sontoku Ninomiya was actually a person who had the disposition to fight against what is commonly known as the Japan Teacher's Union† style of education. He was the embodiment of capitalism. He thought, "If you study hard, you'll eventually be able to make a lot of money and succeed in business." He was a person who tied studying and making money.

The spirit of Sontoku Ninomiya will be extremely important for school education from now on. If teachers can motivate students to study and lead them to a way of thinking that allows them to succeed in business, schools will contribute much to society. If schools can be like that, then the government using tax money to invest in school-related matters would actually be a good thing.

---

* A political party founded by the author in 2009. Since its establishment, it has been consistently advocating what Japan and the world should be from a political viewpoint.

† A major labor union of public school teachers in Japan. Upholds left-wing ideology. Committed members are often criticized for their education based on anti-patriotism and masochistic view of Japanese history.

On the contrary, if we invest taxes into schools to have children work hard in their classes but end up becoming poor, or starting companies that can't pay taxes or starting companies that go bankrupt, then that would be a meaningless investment. Education that simply creates these kinds of people is a problem.

There's no way that a person will be wealthy if he's taught that things like rising up in status and up the career ladder or increasing income and assets are evil. Or, if someone is taught that becoming a company president, becoming a major entrepreneur or becoming a capitalist are evil things, then won't that limit him from ever becoming any of those things?

If someone is told, "You'll go to Hell if you become a company president," then that person wouldn't become a company president. He would only say, "Just place me as a standard employee, please." No one would want to get in a higher position if people are constantly exposed to the teaching, "All standard employees go to Heaven. All company presidents and important executives go to Hell, "because going to Hell is scary. We need to stop thinking like that and get more people to start working to make the world a better place.

Looking at things in terms of companies, we need people who can hire many employees, pay those people salaries and make life worth living for countless people. It's a very good thing for someone to move up in position and become a major executive or company president if he's the type of person who can make his company into a place where the employees are grateful for their experiences there. It's a very good thing if the employees there say things like, "I'm glad I worked for this company. I really felt motivated to work and felt like my life was worth living. The company itself kept growing and making the world a better place. I was really happy about that. I lived a wonderful life." We must aim to become this way. In order to do that, the spirit of an entrepreneur must be cultivated in children, starting from education in schools.

I'm not against the very idea of the government giving subsidies to education. I think it's fine to put that money out there. It's just that if the education is headed in the wrong direction, there's a chance of those subsidies going to complete waste. So, I want people to change their way of thinking.

If the government uses taxes to implement creative education and education with high added value in order to cultivate excellent people who provide good services, make the world a more convenient place and do jobs that are appreciated by the people, then those taxes would be meaningful. It would be a meaningful investment. On the other hand, no matter how much money you insert into something, it would be a complete waste if it merely disappears into thin air.

Looking at the overall state of school education now, it doesn't seem to be promising at all. Due to that, Happy Science, although being a religion, also provides what's called "continuing education for adults." We also provide education for children as well at "Success No.1*" Buddha's Truth prep school for elementary, junior high and high school students and the Happy Science Academy, a combined junior high school and high school.

My wish is to be able to cultivate as many people as possible who can adopt a way of thinking that increases the total amount of national wealth or the wealth in the world, in order to save poor people in this world.

The ultra-inspiring quotes of Napoleon Hill

You must all think deeply about "The Law of Similar Wavelengths' Attraction" that I spoke of earlier and strive to maintain a way of thinking that the spirits of poverty despise. You must affirm wealth used for good cause as a good thing, since wealth can buy time and nurture many people. In addition to that, you must cultivate your

---

* See the *About Happy Science* section near the end of this book.

individual character by having a bright and enthusiastic way of thinking, a positive way of thinking and a constructive way of thinking.

You should stop thinking long and hard about bad things. You shouldn't repeatedly think negative things for a long period of time, like a cow chewing the cud. Cows have four stomachs. They can't digest the grass they eat without passing it through four stomachs, but human beings don't and shouldn't have four "stomachs" to slowly go over all of their failures and humiliations. You have to just wash away all of those thoughts from your life. You shouldn't spend your life repeatedly thinking over and over again, for decades, about negative things and worries, about your own failures and things you're sad about.

Happy Science has "Prayer to Drive Out Spirits of Poverty" under the spiritual guidance of Napoleon Hill. One of the famous quotes by Napoleon Hill when he was still alive goes something like this: "If you continue trying even after failing three times, you have the capacity to be a leader. If you keep on trying even after failing ten times, you have the nature of a genius." These words are truly inspiring.

If you are an inventor, then you should not quit, at the very least, after failing about ten times. If you tend to quit after three times, or even after just one time, then you probably won't be able to become an inventor.

But the same thing is actually true for entrepreneurs. I believe they fail many times. However, you can't become an entrepreneur unless you keep repeating the trial and error process.

If one failure completely knocks you out to the point where you can no longer even move, then that would be the end. But don't forget Napoleon Hill's words which mean, "If you continue trying even after failing three times, you have the capacity to be a leader. If you keep fighting without giving up even after failing ten times, you have the nature of a genius."

The Happiness Realization Party can't stop its political activities after hearing those words. Experiencing defeat in the national elections just twice means that we still don't have the capacity to be leaders. If we lose one more time, we'll finally have the capacity to be leaders. And if we lose ten times, we could become political geniuses. The thing is, it's difficult to lose ten times.

I've had a way of thinking similar to the quote from Napoleon Hill ever since I was young, so I'm not afraid of failure at all. I want to live the kind of life where I look at all failures as chances to learn and use them all as springboards or ideas to improve myself even more. I've experienced a lot of success to date, so I have the right to fail, at least a little. The same is true for all Happy Science believers.

Right now, you probably have some things in your life that aren't going your way, for instance, "The economy is bad," "My job isn't going well" or "I'm having problems with interpersonal relationships." But you'll gain the confidence to work with these things in a positive way if you think to yourself, "If I'm still trying hard even after failing three times, then I have the capacity to be a leader. If I'm still trying hard even after failing ten times, then I could become a genius."

Please bounce back over and over again. You must develop the strength in yourselves to turn the tables on and get yourselves out of adversities. This is extremely important and especially necessary now, in this difficult era of turbulence.

Chapter Three

Prosperity Thinking

1

Use Prosperity Thinking to Break Free from Spirits of Poverty

Your life will change when you can recognize Yourself as a spiritual being more than as A physical being

In this chapter, I would like to speak on the subject of "prosperity thinking."

Looking at the current state of Japan and all of the other nations of the world, I feel that prosperity thinking is the way of thinking needed now. It seems that an ideology that is threatening to plunge the world, including Japan, into unhappiness is rearing its head once more, so I strongly feel we have no choice but to fight a war of ideologies. In other words, I want to fight against the spirit-of-poverty ideology using prosperity thinking.

People in this world place far too little importance on the power of the mind. They usually say, "It's a matter of emotions" or "It's just a matter of how you feel." However, this means people who think in these terms are still worldly. More than 70 to 80 percent of their self-awareness is made up of a view that they are nothing more than a physical being living in the third dimensional, material world. For such people, it is highly likely that even if they have faith, they still only understand about 10, 20 or perhaps 30 percent of their own spiritual selves.

Your life will change when you can recognize yourself as a spiritual being more than as a physical being. Phenomena different from what has been happening to you will also start to occur. This signifies that your worldview has changed.

Happy Science has been making More progress than I expected

Looking back at the slightly more than 25 years that we have walked since the beginning of Happy Science [1986], I can see that the things I pictured in my mind have become a reality. And, in a way, I experienced that things even above and beyond what was in my surface consciousness became a reality.

The things that were actually happening were on a much higher level than the things I had in my surface consciousness at that time. What were in my surface consciousness were the decisions that I had been making based on the education and experience gained since birth, or the knowledge and experience acquired through my career. The reality exceeded my imagination; it went one level further than what I had imagined.

However, I don't think that this was a mere coincidence. It happened because I spoke on the topic of this grand future vision in all sorts of lectures from the very beginning. I could say, "It just took a bit of time for that to become reality."

When we first started out 25 or so years ago, we had a small, one-room office. So, I don't think I would have been able to answer if someone had asked me at that point, "Do you think that your group will eventually blossom into a religion with believers in over 90 countries all over the world?" At that point, I probably did not fully believe that, in the future, I would be giving large-scale lectures or that we would be building shoshinkans and local temples all over. Nor would I have firmly believed that we would be establishing an educational institution or launching our own political party, or that I would be giving lectures in English and promoting missionary work all around the world.

Yes, I did clearly speak of these things. But I know now that there was a part of me that could not really accept that these things would actually happen.

People have more power than they think

What I really feel, time and again, is that people actually have way more power than they think they do. What suppresses this power is "impossible thinking" that is put down on them by other people in the course of carrying out their everyday lives in this world. People teach you and get you accustomed to "limited thinking" such as, "You'll never be able to pull that off, even if you try," "That is impossible" or "There is a limit to that." As a result, what often happens is that this kind of thinking becomes second nature, forming a "smaller you" inside.

This is something that might have occurred due to how your parents educated you. Alternatively, it could have been impressed upon you through the way your teachers at school taught you. Or, in some cases, you might end up in this way from what your friends, coworkers or superiors at work tell you after you have gone out into the world. In particular, this country we call Japan has a culture of "tall trees catch much wind," which means that there is a trend of not being able to think big. Just as the word *bubble* implies, there is a tendency to think of having big ideas as being somehow wrong, as being something grand and beyond our abilities to handle.

However, as far as I have seen every person who succeeded had the habit to think, "What do I need to do to make myself big?" and believed that he could do it. I think only people who thought in that way were able to actually express success.

I cannot deny that, due to the influence of things like the education I acquired in this life, it took a bit of time to get comfortable with a spiritual way of thinking. So, a warm-up period was necessary. But I can also say that, in the end, my spiritual self won. When you start spending more time living spiritually than living worldly, your spiritual self gradually becomes your true self.

In March 1987, at my very first lecture session at the Ushigome Public Hall in Tokyo, I gave a lecture entitled, "The Principles of Happiness." On this snowy day, in a lecture hall where about four hundred people gathered, I spoke on the "Fourfold Path" of love, wisdom, self-reflection and progress. Although "The Principles of Happiness" was the title of that lecture, in truth, I simply took my place at the podium without planning the content of my lecture whatsoever. Ever since, for over 25 years, I have continued my practice of giving lectures without planning the content ahead of time. Nevertheless, the things I spoke on in that first lecture session became the ideas that broadly outlined Happy Science thereafter.

In that sense, my lectures are "my words, yet not

my words." What I mean is, the great powers of the heavenly world are helping me carry out my work. This is something that has happened many times in religions of the past as well. But in my case, I have made it clear that the scale is on a level that is higher than anything in the past.

In the past, there were not only language barriers to missionary work, but also things like travel-related barriers and information distribution barriers. Because of this, people could not accomplish an incredible amount of missionary work and teachings only spread through hundreds of years of work.

However, the world has become incredibly convenient now and missionary work is easier. I believe that this means we have reached an era when big things can occur.

Acquire the power of faith in its truest sense

If I may add, there is still an area that is slightly incomplete. This is to say, a great many people have yet to acquire the power of faith in its truest sense. For example, there are many people who limit themselves with materialistic reasons and think, "That is impossible." And there are many people who, when faced with some kind of obstacle or resistance, completely lose their will and energy and are unable to get back up again.

Even so, I have been preaching all over on the topic of "invincible thinking" and ideas like "how to fight in a way that will allow you to get even stronger and not letting sufferings and hardships get in the way." I believe I have been putting this into practice.

By the way, the number of books I have written to date is already over 800*. In the 1980s, a rumor started in the Kanda book district† in Tokyo that said, "This author is going to write 1,000 books in his lifetime." This was right around the time when my spiritual messages series were coming out almost every week. I remember that every now and then, people used to say, "If he keeps going like this, he might actually put out that many books."

After that, in 1991, we were recognized as an official religious corporation and held a massive lecture session at the Tokyo Dome‡. As a result, we were "baptized" by the media, which is to say, we started receiving all sorts of "criticisms of blessing."

Around that time, journalists who were reporting on our organization said, "You need to read 150 books in order to critique Happy Science. It's maddening." I remember someone writing something like, "Stacking up 150 books on my desk and reading them just to do background work for writing a critique allows the content to seep into my head; I was afraid I would end up becoming a believer. The good side, however, was that I could just keep 'consuming' these books nonstop like *Kappa Ebisen*[#], so I was able to successfully work my way through them."

However, after that, I started putting out books with quite difficult content on all sorts of different themes. I started to speak my mind on a multitude of topics. I believe that, in a way, this was a sign that I had been growing.

When we became recognized as an official religious corporation five years after we started in 1986, the feeling of "what it means to be responsible for the entirety of Japan in the true sense" had not fully matured in my mind. At that time, I was just so happy that we succeeded in becoming a religious corporation; I guess my feeling of "wanting everyone in the world to know about this" was stronger. But now, I truly feel responsible for the way this country and the world are. This responsibility I feel has strengthened my desire to do what it takes to push Japan and the world to a better state of being.

---

[*] As of June 2015, the author has published over 1,900 books.

[†] A district of many bookstores and publishing companies.

[‡] An indoor baseball stadium in Tokyo capable of holding 55,000 people. The author delivered 10 lectures there between 1991 and 1995.

[#] A popular Japanese snack. Its advertising copy, *Yamerare-nai, tomara-nai* [Can't stop, won't stop] is well-known.

2

The World Needs the Teachings of Happy Science

Many other countries in the world do not have Prejudice against religion

In the summer of 2011, we built a large local temple in Uganda, which is in Africa. Now, the number of believers in Africa has just exceeded 20,000 people [as of the end of 2011]. I haven't actually been to Africa yet*, but the point is, this is how far our missionary work has come. Also, the number of believers in India has already topped 100,000 and is rapidly climbing up toward 1 million. In this way, our teachings are currently spreading at an amazing rate, in a way that is different from how things are moving along in Japan.

The first people to do missionary work in Uganda were a diplomat couple from Japan. The wife was particularly passionate in her missionary work. She did things like distributing our booklets in English and was responsible for attracting about a hundred new believers. I remember seeing this in a PR video used internally within Happy Science. Right around the time when the number of believers there reached 100 or 200 people, the diplomat couple ended up getting transferred to another country, perhaps because they were so active in their missionary work[†]. In any case, the "genes" to do missionary work took firm root there and now the number of believers has reached 20,000.

In addition, in Malaysia, where I visited on my missionary tour in September 2011, the local believers worked on their own for 10 years and built a local temple. That is something very special. Believers in Brazil also built a shoshinkan on their own. In this way, believers in foreign countries are building their facilities on their own, even when I'm not there to conduct missionary work. In Japan, too, this kind of activity has finally started to expand all over the nation.

While we are extremely cautious, it's also true that we hadn't actually mastered methods for growth in the worldly sense, so that may be why our progress was a bit slow. However, what I've found is, I'm actually becoming more and more convinced that my teachings really are universal and that these teachings are applicable to people all over the world. Even in areas where the ideologies, beliefs, religions and people are different, my teachings touch a common chord. This is a feeling that can't be

---

[*] The author visited Uganda and delivered a lecture entitled, "The Light of New Hope" to thousands of audience in June 2012, eight months after this lecture [which this chapter was based on].

[†] In Japan, missionary activities by civil servants are considered unwelcome.

described. People can understand my teachings, regardless of whether they are Catholic, Protestant, Muslim or Buddhist.

I particularly felt this to be true during my "Asia Mission" [missionary tour in the Asian region] in 2011. First, I visited India and Nepal, known as the birthplace and center of activity of Shakyamuni Buddha [late February to early March]. After that, I visited the Catholic nation of the Philippines and Hong Kong, which has a bit of Buddhism and Taoism but is mainly irreligious [both in May]. Furthermore, I visited the synthetic nation of Singapore, which does not really have any sort of religious presence, as well as the Islamic Malaysia [both in September]. Lastly, I visited Sri Lanka, a nation of Hinayana Buddhism [Theravada Buddhism] [November].

My words immediately resonated with the hearts of the people in each of these countries. I even felt like there were some things that resonated more in those people than in the Japanese people. This is probably because these people don't have prejudice against religion. Unlike the Japanese, these people don't put up a screen between themselves and religion nor approach it with initial suspicion. They believe religion is a good thing. So, most of them approach Happy Science with interest, thinking, "What kind of religion is this?"

I've been preaching since the initial days of our establishment, "The teachings of Happy Science are connected to those of all world religions. We don't deny those religions." This is being proven right now, more than 25 years later. Happy Science will most likely be much more successful overseas than it will be in Japan.

Throw away "smaller thinking" and think bigger

Right now, we are at the stage where we must expand our teachings more and more throughout the world. Therefore, I feel that innovation is needed back home as well. Japanese people particularly have this "island nation attitude" where they have "smaller thinking." Japanese people have the general notion that they aren't anything special. Thus, they only broadcast information abroad on an extremely small scale.

However, the truth is that all sorts of places such as the nations in Asia, Africa and South America actually look up to Japan. They have their eyes firmly set upon us, wondering, "What will Japan do? What will Japan think about that?"

For example, an Iranian person spent two months' worth of salary to fly and attend my lecture session in Malaysia. The price of goods and income in Iran are different from those in Japan, so this person had to spend two months' worth of his salary to come listen to my lecture in Malaysia. Things like this are actually happening right now. The teachings of Happy Science are spreading all over the world.

Also, apparently one out of every two people in Nepal know the name "Ryuho Okawa." This is after I visited Nepal just once. Moreover, I only flew in from Delhi, India to give a lecture and left that same day. I didn't even stay overnight. However, there were huge waves in Nepal because my lecture was broadcasted live nationwide in Nepal via commercial television and public broadcasting and even came out in all sorts of other media.

Furthermore, in Singapore there was a bus with my face painted across it. Compared to this, we can't have such kind of bus running in Tokyo because there are all sorts of strict ordinances and other restrictions.

In this way, things are progressing in the world right now. I really feel that the world needs the teachings of Happy Science, more than we could imagine. For example, this is true of Uganda in Africa, in which civil unrest had been going on for nearly 20 years. Oddly, in Iran we're being told, "Your teachings are the very thing Iran needs right now." The same is true in Malaysia and Brazil. What's more, developed nations like the U.S. and European countries will need these teachings later on, too.

3

Japan is On the Verge of Becoming the World's Role Model

The mission of Japan is to present itself As a new role model

I fully understand the reason why Europe and the U.S. are suffering right now. The U.S., in particular, is trying to become like Japan but is suffering because it can't fully become like Japan. The U.S. is trying to "Japanize" itself but that effort isn't going so well. That's to be expected. The ground that the American culture is built upon is different, so there is no way the U.S. could do the same things Japan does. Even in the Wall Street protests, people keep talking about disparity as is being said in Japan, but they still don't fully understand that this alone won't resolve the problem.

Ultimately, what Japan needs to do now isn't to copy some other country. At this point, there's almost nothing left out there for Japan to copy. It's true that there are some things out there in which other countries are still ahead of Japan. Take space development, for example. There are probably about three or four nations ahead of Japan in this field. Or in terms of military technology, there might be one or two nations out there that are more advanced than Japan. However, the truth is that there are no countries out there for Japan to model in other fields.

The opposite is true, however. There are many nations out there that are working hard to catch up and overtake Japan. We're in an age when we must create the next new role model. This is something to take to heart. In the past, simply copying others was good enough. Now, we can't get by simply copying things that are already out there in the world. Japan must not be afraid to present itself as a new role model.

When I used to work in the U.S. about 30 years ago, everyone said, "Things that are happening in the U.S. will start happening in Japan a decade later." Because of that, it was generally thought that you would succeed if you went to study in the U.S. or if you looked at what happened in the American society and laid the groundwork for that in Japan ahead of time. This was true in fields like the home electronics industry and the automobile industry, too.

However, that era is now well behind us. Japan must be the new role model.

Currently, the EU [European Union], which is comprised of multiple countries in Europe, is also having trouble operating. Greece and other member states are on the verge of bringing down the entire EU. Germany is trying to do what it can to save them, but it hasn't been able to actually do so. On the other hand, the economy of Japan is much stronger than the core EU nations like Germany and France, or even Great Britain. This is how strong Japan is, yet the Japanese people still aren't fully aware of the power they have.

Furthermore, though some analysts say, "China has surpassed Japan in terms of GDP," the truth is, "A nation with 10 times the population of Japan is only now finally operating on the same level as Japan. That is to say, China finally reached the level where 10 Chinese people can work to earn as much as 1 Japanese person." So, there's still quite a bit of difference between Japan and China. This difference is incredible; each Japanese person makes 10 times the amount a Chinese person does. You all probably don't think that you're doing such an amazing job. You probably just live a normal life. Yet, you're earning 10 times that of the Chinese.

Now is the time for Japan to be the role model for the world.

Look at Happy Science and you'll see the future

Where can this new role model be found? Taking an objective view over Japan, I strongly believe that the future is in Happy Science. I can say with confidence, "Look at Happy Science and you'll see the future of Japan. You will see the future of the world." I can understand very much the desire of the people of the world to study the teachings of Happy Science. My books are selling well, even in China. This is because you can get an image of the future and you'll know what you should do if you read my books. This is why my books are being treasured in China, too.

People who study the teachings of Happy Science really are seeing a picture of the future. They're looking at our attempt to create the ideal state of the future society, which is what we're doing now. My goal is to do whatever I can to create a religious nation that can serve as a role model for the rest of the world.

Your spiritual awakening and spiritual Self-awareness will help you to prosper In this world

Allow me to repeat myself. You can't disregard the spiritual aspect if you're trying to establish faith. Of course, you will see many examples of worldly prosperity. People in the world won't be able to understand the importance of religion unless these kinds of visible events occur. But at the root of these things lies something spiritual. In other words, I'm trying to lay the foundations of an ideology which states, "Your spiritual awakening and spiritual self-awareness will help you to prosper in this world."

For example, Sri Lanka is a country of Hinayana Buddhism. Hinayana Buddhism was established by emulating fundamental Buddhism and has been since. Due to this, Sri Lanka has constantly suffered from extreme poverty. Internal strife and conflict never seem to end there, either. This is because the concept of progress is missing in the teachings of Hinayana Buddhism.

In order to supplement this, I preached on the Fourfold Path of "love, wisdom, self-reflection and progress" as the Principles of Happiness. What I did was to introduce the concept of progress into the teachings. Without this, a religion can't be a future-oriented one. I believe we need to make the countries of Hinayana Buddhism change their way of thinking.

The reason why old religions didn't preach about economic principles is because such principles hadn't yet developed enough in the eras when those teachings were preached. That's all. This is why new principles must be taught today, over 2,000 years later. This is what I'd like to tell you.

4

Think Bigger

The origin of prosperity lies in each person. In particular, I want everyone to try to think bigger. As an individual, you need to improve yourself, at least a little. This is what I mean: "Not just your way of thinking as an individual, but all sorts of other things will change, such as your everyday life, the content of what you read, what goes on at your job and relationships with others, including relationships at work." I want you to know, "Natural consequences will follow as you grow more; all sorts of things will change in your life."

This can sometimes bring pain and sadness. For example, if you work at a company and become very good at your field, you might start finding it difficult to stay at that specific company. This kind of thing happens. It can't be prevented. The question is, "Can you bear with this?"

Of course, there are cases when the company itself will compromise and give you the kind of work that's good for your own goals. There are times when a company may change your position, too. However, there are also cases in which you simply can't stay any longer. In this case, you may do things like transferring to a different company or starting your own.

If you do something like this, then obviously the human relationships and interpersonal environment around you will change. "How important can you see yourself to be?" What I mean is, the importance you place on yourself and your self-image can change. This can lead to changes in the scenery around you, one after another.

Naturally, the books you read will change. Your ideas will change. Your behavior will change. The things you say will change. Furthermore, the way the world treats you will change and your income will change, of course. If you change and the way you think changes, you'll acquire the salary and position that correspond to these changes. The world is indeed well made; it'll give each person what that person deserves.

This is why you must not become too attached to the things that you've been accustomed to thus far. When all sorts of things change, you should accept them and think that you have to switch gears.

This is true for myself, too. Recently, I've come to wear a ring when I give lectures. I was too embarrassed to do so 10 years ago, but now I can do it. I have "prosperity thinking", so I can do it with absolutely no problem now. So, my way of thinking is changing, too.

5

Overcome Crises and Create the Future Society

Japan must issue a new way of thinking Appropriate to its power

Japan has been ruled by a government possessed by the spirits of poverty for some time. If things keep going the way they are now, the country of Japan will fall into decline. This is why I believe we must issue a way of thinking that opposes this. Japan has a much larger chance.

The truth is, right now, every nation in the world is facing difficulties. Things are bad in Europe, the U.S. and other countries, too. Even China is on the verge of an imminent bubble burst and is already starting to sink.

Therefore, if Japan can withstand the current situation, overcome disasters caused by an earthquake* and take one more leap forward, it really can end up leading the world. The opportunity is here right now. We must not allow ourselves to shrink away. This is our chance to show the world, "Even if we're hit by major earthquakes, this nation has the power to survive and overcome it." The same is true for the nuclear power plant issue. This is our chance to prove that we can overcome this crisis and create the future society.

From now on, Japan will be the next role model of the world. What other countries did doesn't matter. Japan has to be the role model and show what it would do. We must not return to how things were before. We must push onward. Being the role model takes courage, it comes with pain. However, we must be able to withstand that.

An editorial of a major Japanese newspaper once said, "The protests on Wall Street in New York are claiming that 1% of the people are rich while the other 99% are poor and suffering. We must listen to that 99%." This is the very essence of Marxism. When I read that editorial, I felt like I was reading an editorial from decades ago. If mass media with such an outdated way of thinking are working this hard to support the administration, the nation can only be headed for poverty. We must find a way to break free from this way of thinking.

Japan must issue the next way of thinking appropriate to its current power. This means, "The time has come for the nation of Japan to hold a higher level of power, display leadership and lead the rest of the world." Now isn't the time to close ourselves off from the world. The world needs Japan to be a global leader. You must know this.

---

* Refers to the Great East Japan Earthquake in March 2011.

With respect to the Israel-Iran conflict in the Middle East, the Arabic nations are facing difficulties because the U.S. is wavering in its approach regarding the problems there. The Arabic nations very much want Japan to step in and do what it can to resolve the situation. They feel that Japan is the only nation that can ask the United States to mediate between them and Israel.

This means that if things progress as they are now, war will break out and the only way to avoid that would be to have Japan step in and persuade the U.S. into mediating between the Arabic nations and Israel. The truth is that the situation can change dramatically based on the decision made by the president of the United States alone and, right now, there's no way of knowing just how things would change. This is why they want Japan to speak its opinion on what should be done. The fact that Japan is a nation that can't speak its mind when its opinion is needed so badly, is very sad indeed.

The reality is that, even when the Japanese prime minister went to the U.S. to have talks with the American president in 2011 for example, he was told, "sayonara" after about 30 minutes. The meeting wasn't much more than greetings and small talk. The U.S. government probably thought, "So, he's the third prime minister since the Democratic Party of Japan came into power. But he and his administration are probably all talk and don't have anything to offer. He would probably be replaced by someone else soon anyway."

It's extremely sad that the prime minister of Japan isn't trusted by foreign countries. The government must select someone with a bit more confidence and substance and the prime minister, himself, must be dedicated to being such a person. He should at least be a person generous enough to listen to others' advice.

If you think creatively, ideas will keep coming

Right now, one of the major debates going on in Japan is the issue of tax hike. Japan's financial deficit is large, so obviously I understand why the government wants to increase taxes. Nonetheless, I must ask, "Was the government able to increase taxes right after the Great Kanto Earthquake*?" At that time, was the government actually able to increase taxes to make up for the deficit despite the immense suffering people in the Kanto region were going through? Obviously not. There's no way the government could impose a tax increase when the people were already suffering so much.

---

* The earthquake that shook the Kanto region in September 1923. It had a magnitude of 7.9 and struck around Tokyo and Kanagawa. It caused extensive damage and estimated casualties totaled more than 100,000 people including missing people.

Or, another example is when Japan experienced widespread destruction in WWII. Was the government able to impose a restoration tax to assist with restoration after the war? No. There's absolutely no way the government could've succeeded in doing that. It could never increase taxes when the people are struggling to rebuild the nation from within the barracks.

The same is true this time around. The government is merely using the earthquake as an excuse in its proposal, "increasing taxes to help with the restoration efforts after the earthquake." Japan will be in serious trouble if the government keeps this mistaken idea. Our economically ignorant former prime minister Naoto Kan[*] once caused a panic by claiming, "Japan will be just like Greece." When the nuclear power plant accident occurred in Fukushima, this prime minister supposedly imagined all sorts of scenarios that culminated in the decimation of Tokyo, of our capital, daily.

To this person, I wrote a book that said, "Don't go on a pilgrimage to Shikoku[†]" [*Moshi Kukai ga Minshuto Seiken wo Mitara Nanto Iuka – Kan-san ni Shikoku Junrei wo Kinzuru Ho* (If Kukai Could See the Democratic Party of Japan, What Would He Say? – A law prohibiting Mr. Kan from making a Shikoku pilgrimage) (Tokyo: IRH Press, 2011)]. But after he stepped down as prime minister, he apparently visited temples again, starting from Enmeiji

Temple, the 54th temple on the Shikoku pilgrimage. Kukai is extremely annoyed by this. Even though he said, "I, Kukai, forbid him from going on the Shikoku pilgrimage," he apparently didn't even listen to that and went anyway.

While serving as prime minister, this person thought only of the decimation of the capital every single day. There's no way the situation in Japan would improve if he thought so in his head.

In contrast to this, even when the nuclear power plant accident occurred, I wasn't shaken in the least. The decimation of the capital could never happen. I'm working in Tokyo, so there's no way such a thing could happen here. So, at that time, I thought, "Happy Science is on a mission to become the leader of the world and save the entire human race. There's no way I'd allow the capital to be decimated" and took a firm stance.

Right after the earthquake, a group of students from Happy Science Academy, which is a combined junior high and high school located in the city of Nasu in Tochigi Prefecture, was staying at Tokyo Shoshinkan, one of Happy Science main temples. All of the high school

---

* Naoto Kan [1946-present]: Second prime minister during the Democratic Party of Japan administration. Served from June 2010 to September 2011.

† A pilgrimage of 88 temples in Shikoku for memorial service or religious discipline. This system was established by Kukai [774 835], the founder of Shingon Sect of Buddhism.

freshmen in that group had planned to go to Boston and New York in late March as part of their foreign language experience, but concern over the impact from the nuclear power plant accident led them to come to Tokyo sooner than planned.

Therefore, I thought, "Since you're all in Tokyo, I won't let you off so easily." I gave them some special English training. I said, "This is a great chance, so I'll give you some special training in English conversation before you go to the U.S." and whipped them into shape. I also told them, "There's no use worrying about Japan. None of you can do anything about it anyway, so just go to the U.S. as according to plan. You have to go on with your foreign language experience for the future." With that, I sent them off.

I believe I made the right decision. I was completely unshaken. I didn't worry about anything. In the end, there's nothing you can do if you only think about negative things. Ideas will keep coming if you approach things from a creative stance. You have to realize that you can completely redo things from the bottom up.

Leave behind assets for the future
By making large-scale developments

Basically, I believe the private sector should take the initiative in earthquake restoration. In times like these, instead of deficit bonds, the government should issue 60-year construction bonds or something like that and construct all kinds of things that we weren't able to build in the past.

If you look at other Asian countries right now, their urban areas are fairly impressive. There are many places that are more impressive than Tokyo. This is an embarrassment for Japan. The value of the yen is high right now, so you should take a trip abroad every now and then. It'll make you realize just how sad Tokyo really looks.

In other words, Japan still has many things to do. The Petronas Twin Towers in Malaysia are more impressive than Roppongi Hills* in Tokyo. We must not allow ourselves to be satisfied with the current Roppongi Hills. We must build something even bigger.

One tower of the Petronas Twin Towers was constructed by a Japanese consortium and the other by a South Korean consortium. The fact that we can build

---

* One of the biggest and most popular commercial complexes in Tokyo. Built in 2003.

something that amazing in another country, but not here in Japan, is truly embarrassing. Shinagawa Station in Tokyo is still only two stories high. This must be some kind of joke. Kyoto and Nagoya Stations have high-rise hotels built on top of them. In contrast, Shinagawa Station still has plenty of unused assets, which is truly a waste. I want to say, "Do your job."

Japan is a creditor nation with a lot of credit, so we can convert that into money as much as we want. Japan can still invest a lot more. It's the government that's in debt; the people are the creditors, so there are no problems for us at all. "Forcing our debt on future generations" is a grave misunderstanding. In order to leave assets behind for the future, or in order to leave behind assets to our descendants, we need to make large-scale developments right now. You must realize that we can and should do so right now.

As long as Happy Science exists, Japan will only prosper

We shouldn't allow things like earthquakes to scare us. The strength of Japan is being tested right now. An earthquake with a magnitude of 9.0 is not going to destroy the entire nation. Instead, we should use this as a springboard and think of ways to build up the Tohoku region, which was previously underdeveloped. We have to build up enough strength to be able to dive immediately into restoration in case earthquakes hit other regions in the future.

Look at Kobe. When an earthquake struck there in 1995, everyone wondered, "Is this the end of Kobe?" But right now it's prospering very strongly. This is the strength of Japan. I believe in that strength.

Happy Science is a religion that preaches teachings that serve as the center of support of this prosperity. As long as Happy Science prospers, grows and continues expanding, Japan will only prosper. We should be very much aware that we have the obligation to become the leaders of the world. This is my resolve now, after 25-plus years since the start of Happy Science.

Chapter Four

Become Closer toward the God of Prosperity

1

Hiroshima's Impact on Japan

Hiroshima, the beginning of my temple visits

On February 26, 2007, I started visiting Happy Science local temple all over Japan. The first place I went to was Hiroshima. In this sense, I have a deep emotion toward this city.

In the beginning, some were opposed to the idea that the head of our religion should go through the trouble of visiting all the different temples. So, opinions were divided. But in the end, although it was not an easy quest, I visited Happy Science temples for over four years till October 2011.

During this time, I gave over 600 lectures including those outside Happy Science temples. I also wrote several hundred books to add to my collection and went abroad more than before. My lecture venues abroad have become huge. Sometimes they pitched tents around the podium in enormous fields. There are so many people who want to attend my lectures these days; they can no longer find buildings large enough to fit them.

All in all, I feel that as a religion, we did the right

thing during those four years. And it all started from Hiroshima.

Original sins born in Hiroshima:
The allergy against nuclear energy and
The yutori *education* [*] *system*

In my opinion, there are two things originally from Hiroshima that had a major impact on entire Japan.

One is the Japanese allergy against nuclear power that started in Hiroshima as a consequence of the A-bomb disaster.

The Tohoku earthquake and tsunami that damaged reactors in Fukushima may have triggered the nuclear power syndrome throughout Japan. However, the Japanese sensitivity toward all things nuclear is an older trauma that has strongly influenced people's reaction. This is the first thing from Hiroshima that has had a major impact on Japan as a whole.

The other thing is the so-called yutori or "pressure free" education system. The yutori education system

[*] An experience-oriented and lenient educational policy that contained less school hours and curriculum content. The policy was established as a result of criticisms which said that conventional, knowledge-oriented education brought about excessive competition and led to bullying, truancy and delinquency in schools. The current education is conducted under a different policy.

originated in Hiroshima in the 1990s. I'm from Shikoku, but a lot of school principals in Tokushima Prefecture were graduates of Hiroshima University. Hiroshima Prefecture used to be famous for its high-level education.

However, in the early '90s, when somebody from the Ministry of Education [currently the Ministry of Education, Culture, Sports, Science and Technology] went to Hiroshima and became head of the local Board of Education, he introduced the yutori education system and it started spreading across the whole country. As a result, Japan's international competitiveness has dropped significantly and Japan has been stagnant since then, for more than a decade.

Prior to that, Japan had maintained one of the highest educational standards in the world, but academic achievements have dropped considerably in all subjects since the introduction of the yutori education system. Those who proposed the system obviously did not think far enough to realize that students who were subjected to this system at school would end up lowering competitiveness in businesses once they entered the job market.

They thought it was enough to just solve the problems the schools were struggling with. But to put it bluntly, they did not understand that keeping the standards high in our education system raises the level of education itself, which in turn raises the standards of Japanese businesses and maintains Japan's international competitiveness. They thought that as long as things go well in schools, everything would be fine.

I believe these are the two areas in which Hiroshima has had a major impact on the rest of Japan. Of course, the A-bomb was not Hiroshima's fault. It was not as if the people of Hiroshima made an A-bomb and dropped it on their own city, so they are not responsible for this event. How they evaluate the attack, however, is their choice. What I do not want is for this idea to head in a direction strongly against modern civilization that the left-wing factions make it a source of their attack.

In a way, if the people of Hiroshima want to get the entire country involved in the devastation brought to their city by the A-bomb, in other words, if they are still bearing a grudge against the dropping of the A-bomb and are trying to lead others into feeling the same way, then this is a problem.

As for the issue of education, I think it was simply shortsighted to think that problems like bullying and classrooms falling apart could be solved by making things so easy that anybody could get good grades. As a result, more children had to attend cram schools. Unfortunately, even though they attended cram schools, the level of basic knowledge learned in school dropped and therefore the level of cram schools dropped. Now, the burden on children has gotten heavier and the financial burden on households has gotten heavier while Japan's international competitiveness has gone down.

Those who proposed the yutori education system apparently forgot that education was what allowed Japan to achieve such amazing growth after the war. We must not forget this. The rapid modernization process Japan achieved during the Meiji Restoration was also possible thanks to the fact people attended cram schools and other educational institutions and dedicated themselves to their studies, since the later years of Edo period. We should never forget that this educational tradition was the reason Japan did not end up like other Asian countries.

These two problems can be called the "original sins" Japan inherited from Hiroshima. This is why I believe it would be best to start fixing these problems in Hiroshima.

Unlike the Western powers, Japan promoted development where it ruled

Many Japanese feel guilt and regret about Japan's actions in WWII and, to a certain extent, they have reasons to feel this way. However, there are always two sides to the story. It is not always true that the countries that emerged victorious are right.

I visited many Asian countries on my lecture tour through Asia and recently, I have felt the following way. In WWII, about 3 million Japanese perished. Japan had a population of about 80 million at the time the war started. Out of those, 3 million died in the war.

Whenever I visit a foreign country for a lecture, I read up on it beforehand. I have read about the history of other Asian countries and learned that some were under European colonial rule for hundreds of years. The period in which Japan ruled over those countries was short in comparison to that.

The Europeans had no interest in the happiness of the Asian people. In most cases, all they wanted was to import raw materials to Europe for local consumption. Britain ruled India for about 150 years, for example, during which India saw almost no progress. The same is true for other countries. Countries colonized by European powers saw very little progress.

In some ways, Japan behaved similarly to the Western colonial powers, but Japan actively built up infrastructure and educated people in the countries under rule. Consequently, many of these countries saw progress.

Maybe some would see this as a lame excuse, but

it is a fact that there were also people in Japan back then who wanted to bring happiness to other Asians. Look at Taiwan, for example. When Japan ruled Taiwan, Japan sent great people like Inazo Nitobe* and Shinpei Goto†, who later became the mayor of Tokyo, to Taiwan. Japan sent top-level people to Taiwan to promote local development. This is why I think Japan is different from the Western powers.

I also went to the Philippines to give a lecture there [May 21st, 2011]. But I did not feel any resentment toward Japan, at all, from the people. I actually got the impression that the Filipinos had great respect for the Japanese. They seemed to think their country's progress had slowed down because the Japanese were defeated by the Americans, in WWII, after defeating them once in the Philippines.

I don't think regret and guilt are the only feelings the Japanese should harbor in connection with WWII. We need to realize that the Japanese also did good things. In addition, many of the Shinto gods seriously considered liberating the Western colonies.

What our ancestors practiced was definitely not fascism. We were not like the Nazis who killed 6 million Jews. Maybe those who dropped A-bombs on Japan still put Japan in the same basket as the Nazis. However, even the high spirits in the Spirit World tell us that there were big differences between the two. I would like to make this clear.

Hitler, the leader of a defeated nation, went to Hell, but so did Stalin, the leader of a victorious nation. Japan was also defeated, but we know for fact that Emperor Showa[‡] who ruled Japan at the time went back to *Takamagahara*[#]. I believe there was a reason the Japanese Imperial Family survived the war.

It is no use arguing that Japan did not secure world leadership before the war, but I think it is a shame that in today's post-bubble, navigator-less world, Japan still is not a leading global power. I strongly feel that Japan needs to work its way up, become a beacon of light for the world and show people the way.

---

[*] Inazo Nitobe [1862-1933] : educator and philosopher. Served as one of the Under-Secretaries General of the League of Nations. His work, *Bushido : The Soul of Japan* written in English was read by many people in Western countries.

[†] Shinpei Goto [1857-1929]: doctor, cabinet minister and statesman. Served significant posts such as the head of civilian affairs of Taiwan under Japanese rule, the foreign minister and the mayor of Tokyo City.

[‡] Emperor Showa [1901-1989]: the 124th Emperor of Japan. Reigned from 1926 to 1989.

[#] A higher spirit realm in Shintoism where Japanese gods reside.

2

Deny Negative Words and Ideas

People who use pessimistic language are Rarely successful

Here, let me narrow in on the topic of this chapter a little more and talk about the importance of becoming closer toward the God of Prosperity. I will start on a personal level.

People who have a habit of using a lot of negative and pessimistic language are rarely successful. People who always verbalize their personal failures and setbacks, their difficult upbringing and their dissatisfaction or complaint with the present situation are rarely successful, cannot find happiness and never live prosperous lives. This is a law, so please remember it.

The reason these people cannot be successful is that, as they hear their own words, they autosuggest as if those things are true. If they keep giving certain orders, unconsciously, they start behaving in a way that follows those orders. This has to do with the subconscious. People who have a habit of using pessimistic language actually keep giving negative commands to their subconscious, which results in a tendency to be attracted to negative things, dragging the mind further down this negative road.

You should understand that this is a law. If you are frequently using negative language and harboring negative thoughts, you need to deny them. The human mind cannot think of two completely different thoughts at the same time, so you have to decide which option to choose.

Picture a plane and a boat at the same time. It is difficult. Imagine yourself on a plane and on a boat at the same time. Not so easy. You are only going to be able to picture one of these at a time.

Therefore, what's really important is the thought you hold in your mind. If you spend long periods thinking negative thoughts, you will end up feeling negative tendencies and being drawn toward negative things in your life. The reason is that negative people seem like they want to be unhappy. This makes others around such people feel that they want to be treated badly.

Now, it is common in Japan to put people into categories like "S" [for sadist] and "M" [for masochist] or "carnivores" and "herbivores" which respectively refer to aggressive and passive types. In essence, however, all these types attract different things. If somebody is a masochist, people around him develop the desire to bully him; it is his own responsibility to change this. As he seems to be looking for trouble, those around him naturally feel it and start behaving accordingly. As a result, masochists attract trouble.

Some people approach you and make you want to use harsh words on them, while others make it impossible for you to use harsh language on them. Some look like they want to be abused and make you feel like abusing them. Others look impossible for you to say anything offensive to them, as if they repel such things. Some people get bullied and think, "Here we go. I got bullied. Something must be wrong with me." They confirm in their own mind that they are this kind of person and must therefore be somebody who likes to be bullied.

However, this only shows their lack of understanding that their own thoughts are the reason for what is happening to them. They simply do not know how to control their thoughts. So, please make efforts to control and shift your mind.

Do not worry too much about the minor details, But instead cover the main points

I am not just talking about other people here. I had the same negative tendencies when I was about 20. Today, people call me "God of the Earth," so it is not easy for me to talk about my past. Nevertheless, I had rather masochistic tendencies from my late teens until early twenties. Small things would take up a huge portion of my mind and I would think negatively about myself.

Part of the reason was that I was studying for my entrance exams. I was overwhelmed by the demerit system [a Japanese mentality where heavier emphasis is placed on mistakes rather than points earned]; tiny mistakes felt like the end of the world to me. Most of those who went through long periods of preparation for their entrance exams or who did well academically are overwhelmed by such traps and have a tendency to perceive things as great tragedies in their lives. Academically talented students who go through the entrance exam system have a strong tendency to develop a pessimistic attitude. What they fret about is usually no big deal. It is never a life-or-death issue.

There are many Happy Science staff members who are graduates of famous universities. When I look at them, I often think, "He is incredibly smart, so why does he have problems getting things right at work?" Such people have a tendency to focus too much on the minor details. People like him are so afraid of making a small mistake that they focus all their attention on not making this negligible mistake rather than devoting their energy to the main point, which is more important.

If people do this, their job performance will never

improve. They are constantly distracted by small things. If these are not perfect, they cannot bring up a proposal, get their job done or advance to the next step. This makes them very inefficient workers.

These people have not internalized the Pareto principle [the 80-20 rule], which states that if you focus on getting the crucial 20% right, 80% of the job are done. They do not understand that 20% are the vital part of the project and that if they focus on getting this part done, they have 80% of the work covered.

If a company has 100 clients, for example, in many cases it derives 80% of its sales volume from 20 of its clients. This means that, as long as the company makes sure to take care of its 20 most important clients, there will be less pressure on the rest of their work. However, people who do not understand this principle do the opposite and end up expending all their efforts on the clients that bring the smallest sales volume, while neglecting their weightier, more important clients.

Companies with poor business performance have people like this, even in top management positions. Especially, smart students who go through the entrance exam system are often unable to focus on the important part, so they need to be careful. This is something people will never learn unless someone tells them about it.

Being able to be brief, but grasping the important part is not something that is taught in school. People need to learn this once they enter the work force. Somebody needs to tell them that they need to be bold in the working world.

3

Two Airlines, Two Kinds of Service

Are you really looking at things from Your customers' perspective?

I repeatedly say this when I give lectures on management: in a work environment, it is essential to be able to think about things from your partners' perspective or your customers' perspective. Of course, theoretically, you can easily teach this in lectures, but in reality, it is difficult to practice. It is difficult to develop your imagination and employ your creativity enough to be able to put yourself in your customers' shoes. Obviously, all businesses intend to take this stance toward their customers, but most simply end up putting their own ideas into practice.

Do not think that looking at things from a customer's point of view is easy. Many times, businesses want to do things for their customers and put their customers first, but in reality, they do not actually put this into practice.

Another mistake I see a lot is that people think their own company is the best in the country without knowing their peer businesses well. Please be careful about this.

Surprising service of Singapore Airlines

In September 2011, I went to give lectures in Singapore and Malaysia. First, I went to Singapore using Singapore Airlines. This airline is famous for its good service.

Maybe you have heard about it, but on board, slim cabin attendants in ethnic costumes pamper you. Their ethnic costumes are tight-fit, so people who are not slim cannot wear them. The flight I took from Japan to Singapore took about seven hours; I departed in the morning and arrived at night. I was able to get a high class seat, so I actually managed to get some sleep on the plane, which was unusual. The seats were not the reclining type most planes have, but seats that could be turned upside down into a flat bed, allowing passengers to actually lie down and sleep.

I was amazed because it was the first time I saw this kind of seat. It takes a man's strength to turn the seat into a bed, so there were also male cabin attendants on the plane. And thanks to the fact that I could lie on a horizontal bed on this flight, I felt really good when I arrived in Singapore.

What's more, in some countries, it can take up to one and a half hours till you get your luggage from the plane. In Singapore, when we got off the plane, we were led to a special waiting lounge where we could wait until we got our bags. While we were waiting, they served us afternoon tea sets of black tea of a Singaporean brand, cake and snacks on three-tiered tea stands. Once our luggage arrived, we could just take it, get on a taxi and leave the airport.

This was the service given by Singapore Airlines.

Flying with a major Japanese airline

I gave a lecture in Singapore and then we went from there to Malaysia to give another lecture. On the way back from Malaysia to Japan, we used a well-known, major Japanese airline that nearly went out of business later. We used this airline on the way back because its time of departure was more convenient for me.

As I said before, on the Singapore Airlines flight, we departed in the morning and arrived at night, so it was not really a flight we necessarily had to sleep on. In this case, however, we left Malaysia at 11 p.m. local time and arrived in Japan the next morning. There is a time difference of about an hour between Malaysia and Japan. This time, the plane was the oldest I had ever seen. The planes the company uses are under a lease, so our plane probably did not belong to the airline itself, but it really made me think, "Wow, no doubt they got this one cheap!"

The company was in the middle of a management reconstruction process, so I guess it could not be helped. Even so, I had never seen such an old plane before. My seat was so stiff and difficult to move. I had never seen such a stiff passenger seat before. I couldn't believe it. The seat would not move unless I really put a lot of power into it. In addition, three seats were squeezed tightly together to form tiny rows. When I reclined my seat to get some sleep, it hardly moved. I thought, "Seriously? That's it? This is the position I'm supposed to sleep in tonight?"

The chief secretary of Religious Affairs Headquarters at Happy Science, who assisted me on this trip, sat on a seat right next to the wall. He was upset and told me after the flight that when he tried to recline his seat, the wall got in the way and that he had to sleep in the upright position. This was our flight experience with said airline that was trying to implement new management policies, at the time, to stay in business.

During the flight, at around midnight local time, there was an announcement that said, "A typhoon is approaching Japan. It is coming from western Japan and moving toward Tokyo, so we expect some turbulence at dawn." There really was a typhoon ahead. The announcement continued, "Therefore, we will serve breakfast to economy class passengers now."

At that time, it was 12 o'clock midnight, and they probably did this thinking if they didn't serve it then, passengers would fall asleep. They did not want to go through the trouble of waking people up, so they served breakfast before everybody went to sleep. As a result, the economy class passengers got their breakfast at 12 o'clock midnight, Malaysia time. After that, they got nothing else to eat for the rest of the flight due to the turbulence caused by the typhoon.

Business class passengers were served breakfast at 4 a.m. Malaysia time or 5 a.m. Japan time. I think we arrived at around 7 a.m. in Japan, but we got breakfast two hours before that. Maybe some business class passengers managed to get a few hours of sleep before breakfast was served two hours prior to arrival, but economy class passengers were served breakfast before they went to sleep.

So, not only was it a shabby plane, it was also clear they had minimized the number of service staff. They probably served the meal in two shifts, so the same staff could attend to passengers in both economy and business class. It was obvious they had reduced the number of staff to minimize their personnel expenses.

I think this was the result of their management policy. The top management of this company is the type of person who thinks, "If we maximize our sales and minimize our expenses, we can gain maximum profit," so he probably put this philosophy into practice. In short, he decided to borrow a plane on a cheap lease, minimize the number of service staff and drop the quality of service for economy class passengers, making his staff work double shifts.

Stop thinking only about your own company and Holding on to old habits

These were the two airline experiences I had on my way there and on my way back. Going there was great, getting back was terrifying. On my way there, I was able to sleep, felt extremely comfortable and had a really good trip. On my way back, although it was midnight, I had difficulty sleeping, waking up every five minutes, so in the end I probably had less than twenty minutes of sleep in total. That's how bad it was. The difference between the two airlines was huge.

Once you go through something like that, you will choose the better airline whenever you can. Obviously, the Japanese airline was undergoing management reconstruction, so I am sorry to talk poorly about them, but whatever situation your company may be in, you still need to realize that you are competing with other airlines. Be careful not to make the mistake of thinking only about your own company.

Moreover, there was another thing when I got back to Japan. When I walked off the plane with my carry-on, an airline employee picked us up and took us to the waiting lounge. So far so good, but the lounge was more than 1 km [about 0.6 mi] away and she made us walk at a very fast pace. None of my assistants had slept very well on the plane; they said they couldn't walk because they hadn't slept and felt lightheaded as they followed the employee all the way across the airport.

Maybe the airline thought it was giving us VIP treatment, but the employee that showed us the way walked at a rapid pace. She probably walks that fast because she has to make many trips, but it was almost impossible for us to follow her since we hadn't slept very well and were feeling lightheaded as we struggled to walk with our bags.

That was the service the airline gave us. Maybe it thought it was offering us service, but every airline needs to realize that its passengers could compare with other airlines. I'm sorry to speak badly of it since it was in the middle of restructuring at the time, but as I wrote in Chapter 2 of this book, only four of us were allowed into the lounge because there were only four chairs available per group. Thus, one secretary always had to wait outside the lounge. After I mentioned this in a lecture, the airline suddenly started providing extra chairs and, from then on, five people were able to sit together as a group.

Whenever I go on tour within Japan, I take four secretaries with me. So, if the airline tells me, "Only four people per group," one person will always be left out. Mahjong usually requires four people to play and Chinese restaurants may have only four seats per table, but I did not know that airlines had to do the same in their waiting lounges. They would not let all five of us enter although the rest of the lounge was almost empty, simply because it was "company policy." In my eyes, it is not good for a company to say this kind of thing, even if it is nearly broke. That's why I mentioned it in my lecture. Then suddenly, they started supplying extra chairs. I guess someone has connections to the airline.

Service is not a simple matter. If you keep doing things simply because you have always done them in a certain way, you will be unable to change your old habits. You will not be flexible enough to implement changes even when your company experiences trouble.

4

Congratulate Others Rather than Being Jealous

Positive differences emerge through competition

Obviously, differences emerge because there is competition between peer businesses in today's free market economy. Some businesses attract customers and are profitable, while others keep customers away and are not profitable.

At the moment, there is a tendency to see differences as something negative, but generally speaking, I do not think all differences are bad. As long as there is competition, differences will arise; some of those are good. There may be bad differences, but there are also good ones.

If two businesses are doing the same thing, any difference that emerges will usually be bad. But if one business starts doing something different, it is only natural for differences to arise. These differences are the differences in value added. I believe it is a good thing for businesses and individuals to work hard and make progress or make money.

If an airline manages to give customers a comfortable flight experience, for example, then it has done a good job. It is not a bad thing for an airline to increase its revenue as a result of doing that. This is the point we need to be careful about.

At the moment, the media are crying wolf, saying such things as "the global crisis is here" and "the world will soon be in an economic depression." In the fall of 2011, for example, protesters decrying inequality occupied Wall Street in the United States. Later, some Japanese left-wing papers happily reported that the movement had spread to over 80 countries in the world. However, I believe the philosophy these protests are based on is dangerous. It is wrong to believe that all differences are bad.

Differences should emerge between businesses when it comes to customer service, for instance, and for this to happen, we need businesses to compete. It is important to have competition because then, only the businesses able to make a profit by supplying good services will survive the selection process. In a competitive situation, companies that feel like their peer companies are going to get ahead of them will work hard to catch up. We need to understand this and avoid falling for misguided ideologies.

If the outcome is the same no matter what you do, everything would degrade. We should do our best to ensure equal opportunities for everyone, but if we fail to accept that this will lead to different outcomes, we will never prosper.

We can't call it professional baseball
If there were no "inequality"

Look at professional baseball, for example. Imagine if all batters with a batting average of over .300 were to be fined! In professional baseball, there is a huge difference in salary between a player hitting at .300 or slightly below it at .290. Looking at the numbers, the batting averages do not seem to differ much, but in reality, reaching the .300 target or not makes a huge difference.

Perhaps you could imagine players who hit more than 20 home runs would get fined 10 million yen [$100,000]* for each home run. This would be unbearable for home run hitters. It would be easier for players to avoid home runs; hitting them is much more difficult. Try hitting a home run. It is tough to do and takes a lot of effort. This is why regarding differences as something negative and telling all players to lower their skill levels downward to the average is like putting the cart before the horse.

We can't call it professional baseball if we had rules saying things like, "Nobody is allowed to hit more than five home runs a year," "No batting averages higher than .300" and "Since batters with a batting average under .200 have the risk of getting fired, pitchers are obliged to throw them easy balls." In such a scenario, players would no longer do their best. Nobody would want to pay money to watch baseball games.

Ichiro[†] is getting paid a huge salary because he hits drives and gets on base. This can be considered "inequality" of course, but it was his personal efforts and talent that have taken him to where he is now. In that process, he has gained many enthusiastic fans that love what he does and get pleasure out of it. We must affirm this kind of inequality.

It is Ichiro's personal matter what he does with the money earned. If he uses it for gambling and other morally questionable things, his popularity will fall and he will earn just punishment for his mistakes. But he has been known to decline the People's Honor Award in the past, so he obviously has the ability to be quite strict with himself and is unlikely to go down the drain so easily.

Getting back to the point, we need to understand that there are good differences. Be careful about the kind of ideology that stamps all differences as bad. You should be on your guard, especially when people confuse jealousy with justice. Jealousy could build up and possibly be

---

[*] Assuming USD to JPY exchange rate at $1=¥100

[†] Ichiro Suzuki [1973-present]: Japanese baseball player (outfielder). Turned professional in 1992 and has been playing in Major League Baseball [MLB] since 2001 (Seattle Mariners, New York Yankees and Miami Marlins). Set many records, such as 4,000 hits in his professional baseball career.

declared justice in a society, but not a single person can find happiness as a result of that. Please keep this in mind.

If profits are deemed bad, then there will only be deficits. As a consequence, nobody will be able to pay taxes. This is a dangerous tendency.

As I have said many times before, we need to have the heart to congratulate others in order to fight jealousy. Successful people have earned their success by coming up with ideas, working hard and applying themselves to their goals, so we should congratulate such people. We should think, "I want to follow him." This is how you can get closer to the people you admire. If you have a tendency to have negative and envious feelings toward successful people, you need to control those emotions.

5

Love the God of Prosperity, Not Spirits of Poverty

"Time is money" is true, but so is "money is time"

When I was young, a part of me thought opposite to a prosperous way of thinking. Many religions, at least in their primitive stages, also see money as a bad thing. Religious people tend to think this way; they are relatively more attracted to honorable poverty. This is the idea that says, "The poor are right and the rich are mistaken."

In reality, it is difficult to succeed in business. You cannot generate revenue if you do not earn the support of many people and get many people to buy your products or use your services. Additionally, if the person managing the business is corrupt, customers will stay away from him and his business. Businesses are judged by the strictest standards. It is important to be aware of this.

Another important point is the way you use time. Benjamin Franklin said, "Time is money." It's true that the way we use time is expressed in the money we make as a result. Everybody has the same amount of time; there are 24 hours in a day and human life usually lasts slightly less than a hundred years. However, it is a long established fact that depending on how people use their time, some become prosperous while others do not. To put it simply, your life can turn out completely different depending on how you use the 24 hours in a day.

In other words, the reverse expression, "Money is time" also holds true. As I wrote in Chapter 1 of this book, I realized this when I was young. The reason this holds true is that if you have money, you can buy time.

We, Happy Science, are putting this principle into practice, so I know this very well. With money, we can build shojas, advance our missionary work abroad and build schools. But if we could only manage to collect money slowly, it will take much longer to make progress regarding these activities. Consequently, "Money is time" is also true.

You cannot get something if you reject it

Money itself is neutral, so what matters is what objective you have in mind when using it. Obviously, we should avoid letting it fall into the hands of bad people and make sure it gets used by good people. I hope that companies trying to make the world a better place will prosper as much as possible. I do not teach, "If you make money, you will go to Hell." Be careful about this kind of ideology.

If you reject wealth in your subconscious, you are unlikely to become successful as an entrepreneur. You cannot get something if you reject it. If you reject wealth and think that accumulating it amounts to exploitation, that's where you have a problem.

Prime Minister Noda* [at the time of the lecture] won first place in something not very honorable. On October 14, 2011, the Noda cabinet made an announcement revealing the assets owned by different cabinet members. A detailed report published in the paper the next day stated that Prime Minister Noda was the poorest Japanese prime minister at the point of taking office since the government started disclosing assets of cabinet members and their families back in 1989. He owned land and buildings in Chiba Prefecture in addition to his savings of over 2 million yen [$20,000], which came out to a total of more than 17 million yen [$170,000] in assets. But he also had housing loans and other debts which amounted to nearly 34 million yen [$340,000]. This meant he had a deficit of slightly less than 20 million yen [$200,000].

This is very similar to Japan's financial situation at the moment, so I suspect he looks at our national finances

---

* Yoshihiko Noda [1957-present]: third and last prime minister during the Democratic Party of Japan administration. Served from September 2011 to December 2012.

the same way he looks at his own finances. I would say he is not very good with money despite being a student of Konosuke Matsushita*. In my opinion, I do not want to see my country managed by a man who has a pile of debt in his private life. I would like somebody who is good at managing finances and is able to at least keep a positive balance on his private accounts to run the country.

What is even more important is how the top leaders of countries think. If they embrace the kind of ideology that sees wealth as something negative and deficits as something good, that is dangerous. If a country's top leader does away with the idea of prosperous thinking, all the people of that country will end up getting possessed by spirits of poverty.

I can see traces of this tendency in President Obama, too. In this sense, he is like the former Japanese Prime Minister Kan. President Obama graduated from Harvard and then worked as a volunteer lawyer in a poor area of Chicago. Obviously, this was his choice; he has the freedom of thought and belief. Other top graduates from Harvard work at Wall Street and earn huge salaries, which he obviously does not like.

He keeps attacking these people and I feel this is due to personal reasons. Perhaps he tried to get into

---

* Konosuke Matsushita [1894-1989]: a late business manager who founded and established Matsushita Electric Industrial Company (now called Panasonic). In his later years, Matsushita devoted himself to raising many politicians.

some company at one point and failed. I don't know, but I think he is trying to blame others for his personal economic failure. Saying most people are poor only because one small part of the population is rich is a convenient excuse if policymakers are trying to shift the blame away from themselves. It seems as if President Obama is using this excuse.

Stop fighting over pieces of a pie and Create wealth instead

You should love the god of prosperity, not spirits of poverty. Please think in the following way. Prosperity is good for the world. The more prosperous you are the more people you can help and the more you can contribute to world's progress. It is no good for more and more people to fall in love with the idea of poverty. A society in which rich people are slammed by the jealousy of many others is no good.

Even if Ichiro makes a billion yen a year, a society where people would drag him across the baseball field and beat him to death with a baseball bat would be horrible. If you are jealous, go to the batting cage and start practicing. Start practicing from elementary school or junior high school. If you are not prepared to do that, you have no right to be jealous.

It is easy to feel jealous, but rather than verbalizing them, praise the people you tend to feel jealous of and try to emulate what they are doing. Follow their example and use this driving force to help yourself get even a step further in your own life. This is the attitude you should have. If you do not make an effort to produce as many wealthy individuals as possible, society as a whole will not flourish.

If you keep nurturing the idea that the pie is never going to get bigger and that all you can do is to fight over the pieces, this will be a world governed by the law of the jungle. Instead, you have to think about creating wealth. You have to think of ways that would bring prosperity to the masses.

In the end, there is only one way of doing this.

Invent products the world has never seen. Create things the majority of people would enjoy. If you continue doing this kind of work, there will definitely be progress. This is how things work; this is the mechanism. There is nothing difficult about it.

However, if you keep making decisions from a selfish perspective, your perspective will become skewed and you will make the wrong decisions. You must strongly push the idea of prosperity especially when a country seems to be ruled by a "government of poverty."

Afterword

The world economy has gone beyond stagnation and is now on the verge of a recession or, rather, a great depression. It seems as though Japan is trying to close its doors in the economic sense and heading toward "one-country stability."

A spirit of poverty stands firm in the center of this nation. This spirit has regulated the supply of currency, laid down fiscal austerity measures and is taking the nation toward a "more taxes, deflationary" policy*.

This is Japan's "back-to-the-postwar" culture that refuses to believe in the God of Prosperity. Perhaps politicians and public officials soaked in this culture believe that they can gain more power by making the people poor.

Time is money. Money is time. Speed up the rate of economic progress. Appreciation of yen is a revelation from Heaven to issue more yen. "Inflation fighter" is not in demand during times of deflation. What matters is a culture that appreciates people who get hits and homeruns.

Ryuho Okawa
National Teacher
January 17, 2012

---

* The author mentions here the economic policies in effect in January 2012. Later, the Bank of Japan changed its monetary policy to increase money supply, just as the author suggested.

ABOUT THE AUTHOR

Founder and CEO of Happy Science Group.

Ryuho Okawa was born on July 7th 1956, in Tokushima, Japan. After graduating from the University of Tokyo with a law degree, he joined a Tokyo-based trading house. While working at its New York headquarters, he studied international finance at the Graduate Center of the City University of New York. In 1981, he attained Great Enlightenment and became aware that he is El Cantare with a mission to bring salvation to all humankind.

In 1986, he established Happy Science. It now has members in over 165 countries across the world, with more than 700 branches and temples as well as 10,000 missionary houses around the world.

He has given over 3,450 lectures (of which more than 150 are in English) and published over 3,000 books (of which more than 600 are Spiritual Interview Series), and many are translated into 40 languages. Along with *The Laws of the Sun* and *The Laws Of Messiah*, many of the books have become best sellers or million sellers. To date, Happy Science has produced 25 movies. The original story and original concept were given by the Executive Producer Ryuho Okawa. He has also composed music and written lyrics of over 450 pieces.

Moreover, he is the Founder of Happy Science University and Happy Science Academy (Junior and Senior High School), Founder and President of the Happiness Realization Party, Founder and Honorary Headmaster of Happy Science Institute of Government and Management, Founder of IRH Press Co., Ltd., and the Chairperson of NEW STAR PRODUCTION Co., Ltd. and ARI Production Co., Ltd.

WHAT IS EL CANTARE?

El Cantare means "the Light of the Earth," and is the Supreme God of the Earth who has been guiding humankind since the beginning of Genesis. He is whom Jesus called Father and Muhammad called Allah, and is *Ame-no-Mioya-Gami*, Japanese Father God. Different parts of El Cantare's core consciousness have descended to Earth in the past, once as Alpha and another as Elohim. His branch spirits, such as Shakyamuni Buddha and Hermes, have descended to Earth many times and helped to flourish many civilizations. To unite various religions and to integrate various fields of study in order to build a new civilization on Earth, a part of the core consciousness has descended to Earth as Master Ryuho Okawa.

Alpha is a part of the core consciousness of El Cantare who descended to Earth around 330 million years ago. Alpha preached Earth's Truths to harmonize and unify Earth-born humans and space people who came from other planets.

Elohim is a part of El Cantare's core consciousness who descended to Earth around 150 million years ago. He gave wisdom, mainly on the differences of light and darkness, good and evil.

Ame-no-Mioya-Gami (Japanese Father God) is the Creator God and the Father God who appears in the ancient literature, *Hotsuma Tsutae*. It is believed that He descended on the foothills of Mt. Fuji about 30,000 years ago and built the Fuji dynasty, which is the root of the Japanese civilization. With justice as the central pillar, Ame-no-Mioya-Gami's teachings spread to ancient civilizations of other countries in the world.

Shakyamuni Buddha was born as a prince into the Shakya Clan in India around 2,600 years ago. When he was 29 years old, he renounced the world and sought enlightenment. He later attained Great Enlightenment and founded Buddhism.

Hermes is one of the 12 Olympian gods in Greek mythology, but the spiritual Truth is that he taught the teachings of love and progress around 4,300 years ago that became the origin of the current Western civilization. He is a hero that truly existed.

Ophealis was born in Greece around 6,500 years ago and was the leader who took an expedition to as far as Egypt. He is the God of miracles, prosperity, and arts, and is known as Osiris in the Egyptian mythology.

Rient Arl Croud was born as a king of the ancient Incan Empire around 7,000 years ago and taught about the mysteries of the mind. In the heavenly world, he is responsible for the interactions that take place between various planets.

Thoth was an almighty leader who built the golden age of the Atlantic civilization around 12,000 years ago. In the Egyptian mythology, he is known as god Thoth.

Ra Mu was a leader who built the golden age of the civilization of Mu around 17,000 years ago. As a religious leader and a politician, he ruled by uniting religion and politics.

ABOUT HAPPY SCIENCE

Happy Science is a global movement that empowers individuals to find purpose and spiritual happiness and to share that happiness with their families, societies, and the world. With more than 12 million members around the world, Happy Science aims to increase awareness of spiritual truths and expand our capacity for love, compassion, and joy so that together we can create the kind of world we all wish to live in.

Activities at Happy Science are based on the Principle of Happiness (Love, Wisdom, Self-Reflection, and Progress). This principle embraces worldwide philosophies and beliefs, transcending boundaries of culture and religions.

Love teaches us to give ourselves freely without expecting anything in return; it encompasses giving, nurturing, and forgiving.

Wisdom leads us to the insights of spiritual truths, and opens us to the true meaning of life and the will of God (the universe, the highest power, Buddha).

Self-Reflection brings a mindful, nonjudgmental lens to our thoughts and actions to help us find our truest selves—the essence of our souls—and deepen our connection to the highest power. It helps us attain a clean and peaceful mind and leads us to the right life path.

Progress emphasizes the positive, dynamic aspects of our spiritual growth—actions we can take to manifest and spread happiness around the world. It's a path that not only expands our soul growth, but also furthers the collective potential of the world we live in.

PROGRAMS AND EVENTS

The doors of Happy Science are open to all. We offer a variety of programs and events, including self-exploration and self-growth programs, spiritual seminars, meditation and contemplation sessions, study groups, and book events.

Our programs are designed to:
* Deepen your understanding of your purpose and meaning in life
* Improve your relationships and increase your capacity to love unconditionally
* Attain peace of mind, decrease anxiety and stress, and feel positive
* Gain deeper insights and a broader perspective on the world
* Learn how to overcome life's challenges
  ... and much more.

For more information, visit happy-science.org.

OUR ACTIVITIES

Happy Science does other various activities to provide support for those in need.

◆ **You Are An Angel! General Incorporated Association**

Happy Science has a volunteer network in Japan that encourages and supports children with disabilities as well as their parents and guardians.

◆ **Never Mind School for Truancy**

At 'Never Mind,' we support students who find it very challenging to attend schools in Japan. We also nurture their self-help spirit and power to rebound against obstacles in life based on Master Okawa's teachings and faith.

◆ **"Prevention Against Suicide" Campaign since 2003**

A nationwide campaign to reduce suicides; over 20,000 people commit suicide every year in Japan. "The Suicide Prevention Website-Words of Truth for You-" presents spiritual prescriptions for worries such as depression, lost love, extramarital affairs, bullying and work-related problems, thereby saving many lives.

◆ **Support for Anti-bullying Campaigns**

Happy Science provides support for a group of parents and guardians, Network to Protect Children from Bullying, a general incorporated foundation launched in Japan to end bullying, including those that can even be called a criminal offense. So far, the network received more than 5,000 cases and resolved 90% of them.

- **The Golden Age Scholarship**

  This scholarship is granted to students who can contribute greatly and bring a hopeful future to the world.

- **Success No.1**

  Buddha's Truth Afterschool Academy

  Happy Science has over 180 classrooms throughout Japan and in several cities around the world that focus on afterschool education for children. The education focuses on faith and morals in addition to supporting children's school studies.

- **Angel Plan V**

  For children under the age of kindergarten, Happy Science holds classes for nurturing healthy, positive, and creative boys and girls.

- **Future Stars Training Department**

  The Future Stars Training Department was founded within the Happy Science Media Division with the goal of nurturing talented individuals to become successful in the performing arts and entertainment industry.

- **NEW STAR PRODUCTION Co., Ltd.**

  ARI Production Co., Ltd.

  We have companies to nurture actors and actresses, artists, and vocalists. They are also involved in film production.

CONTACT INFORMATION

Happy Science is a worldwide organization with branches and temples around the globe. For a comprehensive list, visit the worldwide directory at *happy-science.org*. The following are some of the many Happy Science locations:

UNITED STATES AND CANADA

New York
79 Franklin St., New York, NY 10013, USA
Phone: 1-212-343-7972
Fax: 1-212-343-7973
Email: ny@happy-science.org
Website: happyscience-usa.org

New Jersey
66 Hudson St., #2R, Hoboken, NJ 07030, USA
Phone: 1-201-313-0127
Email: nj@happy-science.org
Website: happyscience-usa.org

Chicago
2300 Barrington Rd., Suite #400,
Hoffman Estates, IL 60169, USA
Phone: 1-630-937-3077
Email: chicago@happy-science.org
Website: happyscience-usa.org

Florida
5208 8th St., Zephyrhills, FL 33542, USA
Phone: 1-813-715-0000
Fax: 1-813-715-0010
Email: florida@happy-science.org
Website: happyscience-usa.org

Atlanta
1874 Piedmont Ave., NE Suite 360-C
Atlanta, GA 30324, USA
Phone: 1-404-892-7770
Email: atlanta@happy-science.org
Website: happyscience-usa.org

San Francisco
525 Clinton St.
Redwood City, CA 94062, USA
Phone & Fax: 1-650-363-2777
Email: sf@happy-science.org
Website: happyscience-usa.org

Los Angeles
1590 E. Del Mar Blvd., Pasadena, CA
91106, USA
Phone: 1-626-395-7775
Fax: 1-626-395-7776
Email: la@happy-science.org
Website: happyscience-usa.org

Orange County
16541 Gothard St. Suite 104
Huntington Beach, CA 92647
Phone: 1-714-659-1501
Email: oc@happy-science.org
Website: happyscience-usa.org

San Diego
7841 Balboa Ave. Suite #202
San Diego, CA 92111, USA
Phone: 1-626-395-7775
Fax: 1-626-395-7776
E-mail: sandiego@happy-science.org
Website: happyscience-usa.org

Hawaii
Phone: 1-808-591-9772
Fax: 1-808-591-9776
Email: hi@happy-science.org
Website: happyscience-usa.org

Kauai
3343 Kanakolu Street, Suite 5
Lihue, HI 96766, USA
Phone: 1-808-822-7007
Fax: 1-808-822-6007
Email: kauai-hi@happy-science.org
Website: happyscience-usa.org

Toronto

845 The Queensway
Etobicoke, ON M8Z 1N6, Canada
Phone: 1-416-901-3747
Email: toronto@happy-science.org
Website: happy-science.ca

Vancouver

#201-2607 East 49th Avenue,
Vancouver, BC, V5S 1J9, Canada
Phone: 1-604-437-7735
Fax: 1-604-437-7764
Email: vancouver@happy-science.org
Website: happy-science.ca

INTERNATIONAL

Tokyo

1-6-7 Togoshi, Shinagawa,
Tokyo, 142-0041, Japan
Phone: 81-3-6384-5770
Fax: 81-3-6384-5776
Email: tokyo@happy-science.org
Website: happy-science.org

Seoul

74, Sadang-ro 27-gil,
Dongjak-gu, Seoul, Korea
Phone: 82-2-3478-8777
Fax: 82-2-3478-9777
Email: korea@happy-science.org
Website: happyscience-korea.org

London

3 Margaret St.
London, W1W 8RE United Kingdom
Phone: 44-20-7323-9255
Fax: 44-20-7323-9344
Email: eu@happy-science.org
Website: www.happyscience-uk.org

Taipei

No. 89, Lane 155, Dunhua N. Road,
Songshan District, Taipei City 105, Taiwan
Phone: 886-2-2719-9377
Fax: 886-2-2719-5570
Email: taiwan@happy-science.org
Website: happyscience-tw.org

Sydney

516 Pacific Highway, Lane Cove North,
2066 NSW, Australia
Phone: 61-2-9411-2877
Fax: 61-2-9411-2822
Email: sydney@happy-science.org

Kuala Lumpur

No 22A, Block 2, Jalil Link Jalan Jalil
Jaya 2, Bukit Jalil 57000,
Kuala Lumpur, Malaysia
Phone: 60-3-8998-7877
Fax: 60-3-8998-7977
Email: malaysia@happy-science.org
Website: happyscience.org.my

Sao Paulo

Rua. Domingos de Morais 1154,
Vila Mariana, Sao Paulo SP
CEP 04010-100, Brazil
Phone: 55-11-5088-3800
Email: sp@happy-science.org
Website: happyscience.com.br

Kathmandu

Kathmandu Metropolitan City,
Ward No. 15, Ring Road, Kimdol,
Sitapaila Kathmandu, Nepal
Phone: 977-1-427-2931
Email: nepal@happy-science.org

Jundiai

Rua Congo, 447, Jd. Bonfiglioli
Jundiai-CEP, 13207-340, Brazil
Phone: 55-11-4587-5952
Email: jundiai@happy-science.org

Kampala

Plot 877 Rubaga Road, Kampala
P.O. Box 34130 Kampala, UGANDA
Phone: 256-79-4682-121
Email: uganda@happy-science.org

ABOUT HAPPINESS REALIZATION PARTY

The Happiness Realization Party (HRP) was founded in May 2009 by Master Ryuho Okawa as part of the Happy Science Group. HRP strives to improve the Japanese society, based on three basic political principles of "freedom, democracy, and faith," and let Japan promote individual and public happiness from Asia to the world as a leader nation.

1) Diplomacy and Security: Protecting Freedom, Democracy, and Faith of Japan and the World from China's Totalitarianism

Japan's current defense system is insufficient against China's expanding hegemony and the threat of North Korea's nuclear missiles. Japan, as the leader of Asia, must strengthen its defense power and promote strategic diplomacy together with the nations which share the values of freedom, democracy, and faith. Further, HRP aims to realize world peace under the leadership of Japan, the nation with the spirit of religious tolerance.

2) Economy: Early economic recovery through utilizing the "wisdom of the private sector"

Economy has been damaged severely by the novel coronavirus originated in China. Many companies have been forced into bankruptcy or out of business. What is needed for economic recovery now is not subsidies and regulations by the government, but policies which can utilize the "wisdom of the private sector."

For more information, visit en.hr-party.jp

HAPPY SCIENCE ACADEMY JUNIOR AND SENIOR HIGH SCHOOL

Happy Science Academy Junior and Senior High School is a boarding school founded with the goal of educating the future leaders of the world who can have a big vision, persevere, and take on new challenges.

Currently, there are two campuses in Japan; the Nasu Main Campus in Tochigi Prefecture, founded in 2010, and the Kansai Campus in Shiga Prefecture, founded in 2013.

Nasu Main Campus

Kansai Campus

HAPPY SCIENCE UNIVERSITY

THE FOUNDING SPIRIT AND THE GOAL OF EDUCATION

Based on the founding philosophy of the university, "Exploration of happiness and the creation of a new civilization," education, research and studies will be provided to help students acquire deep understanding grounded in religious belief and advanced expertise with the objectives of producing "great talents of virtue" who can contribute in a broad-ranging way to serve Japan and the international society.

FACULTIES

Faculty of human happiness

Students in this faculty will pursue liberal arts from various perspectives with a multidisciplinary approach, explore and envision an ideal state of human beings and society.

Faculty of successful management

This faculty aims to realize successful management that helps organizations to create value and wealth for society and to contribute to the happiness and the development of management and employees as well as society as a whole.

Faculty of future creation

Students in this faculty study subjects such as political science, journalism, performing arts and artistic expression, and explore and present new political and cultural models based on truth, goodness and beauty.

Faculty of future industry

This faculty aims to nurture engineers who can resolve various issues facing modern civilization from a technological standpoint and contribute to the creation of new industries of the future.

ABOUT HS PRESS

HS Press is an imprint of IRH Press Co., Ltd. IRH Press Co., Ltd., based in Tokyo, was founded in 1987 as a publishing division of Happy Science. IRH Press publishes religious and spiritual books, journals, magazines and also operates broadcast and film production enterprises. For more information, visit *okawabooks.com.*

Follow us on:

f Facebook: Okawa Books   Instagram: OkawaBooks
▶ Youtube: Okawa Books   Twitter: Okawa Books
P Pinterest: Okawa Books   **g** Goodreads: Ryuho Okawa

─── **NEWSLETTER** ───

To receive book related news, promotions and events, please subscribe to our newsletter below.

∞ eepurl.com/bsMeJj

─── **AUDIO / VISUAL MEDIA** ───

YOUTUBE   **PODCAST**

Introduction of Ryuho Okawa's titles; topics ranging from self-help, current affairs, spirituality, religion, and the universe.

BOOKS BY RYUHO OKAWA

THE LAWS OF WISDOM
SHINE YOUR DIAMOND WITHIN

This book guides you along the path on how to acquire wisdom, so that you can break through any wall you are facing or will confront in your life or in your business. By reading this book, you will be able to avoid getting lost in the flood of information and go beyond the level of just amassing knowledge. You will be able to come up with many great ideas, make effective planning and strategy and develop your leadership while receiving good inspiration.

THE LAWS OF PERSEVERANCE
REVERSING YOUR COMMON SENSE

"No matter how much you suffer, the Truth will gradually shine forth as you continue to endure hardships. Therefore, simply strengthen your mind and keep making constant efforts in times of endurance, however ordinary they may be. "

-From Postscript

THE LAWS OF INVINCIBLE LEADERSHIP
AN EMPOWERING GUIDE FOR CONTINUOUS AND LASTING SUCCESS IN BUSINESS AND IN LIFE

Ryuho Okawa shares essential principles for all who wish to become invincible managers and leaders in their fields of work, organizations, societies, and nations. Your keys to becoming an invincible overall winner in life and in business are just pages away.

For a complete list of books, visit okawabooks.com

THE LAWS OF THE SUN

ONE SOURCE, ONE PLANET, ONE PEOPLE

Imagine if you could ask God why he created this world and what spiritual laws he used to shape us—and everything around us. In *The Laws of the Sun*, Ryuho Okawa outlines these laws of the universe and provides a road map for living one's life with greater purpose and meaning.

THE GOLDEN LAWS

HISTORY THROUGH THE EYES OF THE ETERNAL BUDDHA

Throughout history, Great Guiding Spirits of Light have been present on Earth in both the East and the West at crucial points in human history to further our spiritual development. *The Golden Laws* reveals how Divine Plan has been unfolding on Earth, and outlines 5,000 years of the secret history of humankind.

THE NINE DIMENSIONS

UNVEILING THE LAWS OF ETERNITY

This book is a window into the mind of our loving God. When the religions and cultures of the world discover the truth of their common spiritual origin, they will be inspired to accept their differences, come together under faith in God, and build an era of harmony and peaceful progress on Earth.

For a complete list of books, visit okawabooks.com

THINKING FINANCIALLY

PRACTICAL SKILLS OF A CORPORATE STRATEGIST

"As the founder of Happy Science, I attained both spiritual and philosophical enlightenment. Not only that, but my background in international business development and as a management professional — a financial expert at a trading company — have been a great driving force in the progress of this religion."

-From Afterword

THINK BIG!

BE POSITIVE AND BE BRAVE TO ACHIEVE YOUR DREAMS

Think Big! offers the support and encouragement to shift to new ways of thinking and mastering self-discipline. The self-proven approach fosters stability and strength in the challenges each of us faces. In addition to his relatable stories and a motivational voice to keep us going, each chapter builds on the next for concrete methodologies that, when added up, are a track to support your dreams, yourself, and your life.

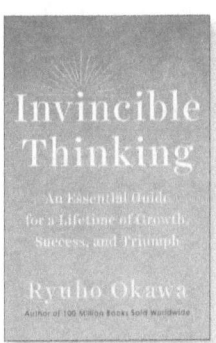

INVINCIBLE THINKING

AN ESSENTIAL GUIDE FOR A LIFETIME OF GROWTH, SUCCESS, AND TRIUMPH

In this book, Ryuho Okawa lays out the principles of invincible thinking that will allow us to achieve long-lasting triumph. This powerful and unique philosophy is not only about becoming successful or achieving our goal in life, but also about building the foundation of life that becomes the basis of our life-long, lasting success and happiness.

For a complete list of books, visit okawabooks.com

MESSAGES FROM HEAVEN

WHAT JESUS, BUDDHA, MOSES, AND
MUHAMMAD WOULD SAY TODAY

If you could speak to Jesus, Buddha, Moses, or
Muhammad, what would you ask? Ryuho Okawa
uses his spiritual power to communicate with
these four spirits and shares their messages to the
people living today.

THE ART OF BUSINESS
REVITALIZATION

MANAGEMENT WISDOM FROM JACK WELCH,
CARLOS GHOSN, AND BILL GATES

In this book, Master Ryuho Okawa conducts
spiritual interviews with three of the greatest
executives of our time. General Electric's Jack
Welch, Renault and Nissan's Carlos Ghosn, and
Microsoft's Bill Gates give readers a glimpse into
how they took hold of opportunities and turned
them into successes.

THE GENIUS OF ICHIRO

THE SECRET BEHIND HIS FOUR THOUSAND HITS

"The words of Ichiro's guardian spirit reveal the
kind of stoicism you would expect of an ascetic or
religious leader. I should probably say no more.
You'll see for yourself as you read what follows."

-From Preface

For a complete list of books, visit okawabooks.com

160

www.ingramcontent.com/pod-product-compliance
Lightning Source LLC
Chambersburg PA
CBHW030302130626
46549CB00002B/649